intimate conversations

intimate conversations

CHRISTIAN SEXUALITY *beyond* PURITY CULTURE

SUSANNAH LARRY

Harrisonburg, Virginia

Herald Press
PO Box 866, Harrisonburg, Virginia 22803
www.HeraldPress.com

Library of Congress Cataloging-in-Publication Data
Names: Larry, Susannah author
Title: Intimate conversations : Christian sexuality beyond purity culture / Susannah Larry.
Description: Harrisonburg, Virginia : Herald Press, [2026] | Includes bibliographical references.
Identifiers: LCCN 2025042029 (print) | LCCN 2025042030 (ebook) | ISBN 9781513816289 paperback | ISBN 9781513816302 ebook
Subjects: LCSH: Sex--Biblical teaching | Sex--Religious aspects--Christianity | BISAC: RELIGION / Christian Living / Family & Relationships | FAMILY & RELATIONSHIPS / Parenting / Motherhood
Classification: LCC BS680.S5 L368 2026 (print) | LCC BS680.S5 (ebook)
LC record available at https://lccn.loc.gov/2025042029
LC ebook record available at https://lccn.loc.gov/2025042030

Study guides are available for many Herald Press titles at www.HeraldPress.com.

INTIMATE CONVERSATIONS

Library of Congress Control Number: 2025042029
International Standard Book Number: 978-1-5138-1628-9 (paperback);
978-1-5138-1630-2 (ebook)
Printed in United States of America

30 29 28 27 26 10 9 8 7 6 5 4 3 2 1

Dedicated to Naun,
for asking questions about the topic
that made me grouchy but also think hard,
but moreover, for washing my dishes
and cleaning my house for half a year
so I could write.

Contents

Foreword

I have a very weird job. It seems like all I do all day, every day, is talk about sex. Our team at Bare Marriage is dedicated to changing the Christian conversation about sex to make it healthy, evidence-based, and biblical, and we do that by conducting huge studies on how evangelical teachings on sex and marriage have affected couples' sexual satisfaction (and especially women's sexual experience). But so often these conversations about sex revolve around trying to repair harm that has already been done.

Every day I see the bad fruit of the conversations we're currently having—or not having. Within the church, almost 50 percent of married Christian men still use porn, even if just occasionally.[1] Evangelical women suffer from twice the rate of sexual pain disorders as those outside the church.[2] We have a 47-point orgasm gap, where 95 percent of married Christian men report they almost always or always orgasm in a given sexual encounter, compared with just 48 percent of women.[3] Even if people do everything right and wait for marriage, we're still not seeing flourishing sex lives.

And whether or not one is married, we're seeing heartache, objectification, and dehumanization, and far too much sexual assault. Indeed, teen girls are more likely to be sexually assaulted in churches that teach modesty messages than in churches that don't. Our conversations about sex so often make things worse, because we're asking the wrong questions.

What would happen if we realized that conversations about sex are not just for teenagers and young adults figuring out what to do about sex before marriage? What if there was recognition that wrestling with our sexuality looks different when you're fourteen or twenty-four or when you're divorced at thirty-four, widowed at fifty-four, or in a stressful marriage at forty-four? Our sexual selves grow and change, and our questions, and search for meaning, shift.

The Christian world desperately needs the conversations that Susannah invites us to have on these pages. And yet the conversations that Christians think we need and the conversations we actually do need are often two different things. Parents want to figure out how to talk to kids about sex so they won't do it, won't think about it, won't get in trouble. Church leaders all too often use our sexual choices to define who is acceptable and who is not. And many on the more progressive side want the conversation to shift so that consent is all that matters, in an effort to stop shame.

Susannah Larry makes a persuasive case in these pages that these are all the wrong starting points, and we need to think bigger. We need to wrestle with questions like "How does my sexual expression reflect my relationship with myself as someone made in the image of God?" and "How can I honor Jesus with my sexuality while also honoring and enjoying my sexuality"? We need to see that our questions about sex must expand beyond just "What does God let me do?" and instead aim for the heart of the gospel. Our sexuality doesn't exist in a vacuum, and sex and our relationship with God and ourselves should all exist together.

We don't just need sexual education. We don't just need sexual rules or boundaries. We need sexual discipleship, and that's what Susannah invites us to.

Wrestle with these questions. Weep over their implications, as I did when reading these pages. But then let something new grow—a glimmer of hope leading to a bigger vision for intimacy, relationship, and even pleasure. That's what God calls us to, and it's time to start talking about it.

—Sheila Wray Gregoire
Founder of Bare Marriage and
coauthor of *The Great Sex Rescue*

Introduction

I'm fascinated that a sacred text including the line "My beloved thrust his hand into the opening, and my inmost being yearned for him" (Song of Songs 5:4) translates into an American Christian culture where parents host purity balls and bestow promise rings. It just doesn't make sense to me. True love may wait, but the lovers of the Song of Songs sure don't.

There has to be a better way to talk about biblical sexuality as Christians, and I'm here to find it. What-goes-where and how-we-get-it-in-there aside, we deserve to wrestle with the mystical connection we have with God, our bodies, ourselves, and others through sexuality. We need to talk about the meta-questions of how we understand ourselves as sexual beings, especially as sexual beings who identify as Christian, and if and how the Bible guides us as we make sexual decisions in our lives.

My deep love for the Bible leads me to write this book. I became a biblical scholar because I grew up to discover that there is so much content in the Bible that shatters the limits of my upbringing. Sex included. I became a writer because there is so much I want to share about *how* the Bible matters in dealing with questions like those about sex—just not, often, in the way people think.

I haven't always been open about the topic of sex. For perspective, when I was eighteen, I had no idea where a tampon went or how to use one, and I may even have claimed to a friend that I lacked the necessary parts. In this, the Christian cultures I grew up around—from both the progressive and evangelical ends of the spectrum—failed me.

I grew up sandwiched between cultures. On one hand, my family homeschooled. That fact, coupled with our in-church-whenever-the-doors-were-open church attendance, might have led an observer to think we were part of the wave of evangelical Christianity that washed over American culture in the 1990s and 2000s, popularized in television shows like *19 Kids and Counting*. Indeed, many of my acquaintances were from those types of families, where having four kids like we did was considered indecently under-fertile. My teammates on the cross-country team that my dad graciously coached for eight-plus years often had families of twelve or fourteen. Uniform shorts that showed some thigh generated parental unrest significant enough to force a parent meeting that concluded with a requirement to wear spandex shorts under the uniform. My friends grew up deep in purity culture, although we didn't have the language for that then, and I experienced the ripples adjacent to its epicenter.

But I was also aware that I was very different from these friends. My parents clarified that we homeschooled not because of religious fundamentalism—evolution, climate change, and gender equality were non-issues in my household—but because my parents believed that the available public schools weren't a great fit for our academic pursuits. We were not, according to our own self-understanding, *those* kind of homeschoolers.

My childhood was rich in everything to prepare me to become a good liberal American. I attended protests of the Afghanistan and Iraq wars when I was eleven and twelve, and went to screenings of documentaries about the corruption of the current Republican administration. One of my first R-rated movies was *Milk* (2008), about the famous gay California politician and activist Harvey Milk. My parents took me to lectures and book signings where I met John Lewis, Madeleine Albright, Jimmy Carter, and even J. K. Rowling (before the exposition of her transphobic views). On election nights, my mom printed out maps for my siblings and me to color in electoral results in red and blue as the returns came in, waiting with bated breath to see if our candidate would win. At dinner, my parents encouraged my siblings and me to discuss politics and religion, and one of my mom's proudest moments was when my older brother described how he had compassionately deflected someone's evangelistic attempts at the park. (In our subset of the local Christian community, such forms of evangelization were viewed with suspicion.) With all that cultural capital of white, upper-middle-class intelligentsia, I was poised to take my place as one of the liberals, or so I thought.

It wasn't really until college that I realized what an anomaly my upbringing was. In terms of my political and religious beliefs, I thought of myself as a liberal. But in terms of my relationship sensibilities, I was more of a conservative. I had zero dating experience. I knew very little about boys (or girls, for that matter). I loved Jesus. I was pretty sure that the Bible had a few things to say about sexuality (though not the antigay rhetoric I'd heard from conservative Christians). I was prepared to "wait until marriage."

Because that value was also something I learned from my family. Though the messaging I received from my elders was rarely specific, there is one particular moment when I remember my sisters and I being told, "What beautiful, intelligent girls you are! And it will be the greatest gift to your husband to save your virginity for him."

I was around thirteen or fourteen at the time I heard this. That moment continues to stand out to me because there was so little discussion of sexuality in my home or church. This "saving virginity for your husband" comment was a complete non sequitur to any prior or subsequent conversation. At that age, I'm frankly not even sure I knew what virginity meant, other than the fact that I wasn't married, kind of like Mary, Jesus' mom. But I remember understanding that virginity was something special, something just for my husband, something I would give to him and him alone. I also know that I internalized how vital it was to wait to have sex with any partner until I was married. In theory, that wasn't a bad concept. But in practice, there was a lot to that encounter that I wish I could edit.

If I could revisit that moment as an adult, I'd push back. As I think back on that message, I'm struck by how much it contradicts the way we were raised to value agency and education. Was our virginity a greater gift to our future husbands than our intellect? Than our compassion? Than our humor? Did we have to get married at all to have fulfilling lives? What if we didn't want to get married? Anyone in my family would have answered no and assured us of our value independent of marriage, I'm sure. My parents raised us to be feminist superstars with advanced degrees who could have options for our financial futures. Still, there were a lot of embedded cultural assumptions when my sisters and I were told to save our virginity for our husbands. The advice we received contained no explicit ties to the Bible or theology to explain to us *why* our virginity was such a prized gift. There was no assumption (explicitly, at least) that our abstinence was also linked to gender hierarchy. The influence of purity culture was there, but insidious and shadowy.

In the 1990s and 2000s, purity culture in evangelical circles boomed with the popularization of old classics like Elisabeth Elliot's *Passion and Purity*. Books like *When God Writes Your Love Story* by Eric Ludy and Leslie Ludy, *And the Bride Wore White* by Dannah Gresh, and *I Kissed Dating Goodbye* by Joshua Harris claimed to hold the recipes for a wedding day where both parties were spotless before God, each other, and their families.[1] "Courtship" among young couples that was chaperoned and parentally curated could replace worldly dating. Young women received purity rings from parents and were presented as debutantes by their fathers at purity balls. (I've heard of young men wearing purity rings, too, but my unscientific impression is that this was less common.) In pulpits, small groups, and biblical counseling sessions, purveyors of purity culture prepared young people to have "biblical marriages" by saving their sexuality for a covenantal bond. I imagine that the most extreme teachings were practiced by a small minority. However, as the term "purity culture" suggests, the influence of these teachings pervaded far beyond their origination points. Even, it turned out, into my self-proclaimed "liberal" household.

Beyond that moment in my early teens, I don't recall any other specific instruction on sexual morality during my youth, either from my family or my church. I found out what sex was by looking up an article in the *World Book Encyclopedia* when I was thirteen, because I'd heard the word before but didn't know what it meant. I then had to look up other words to follow—anatomical terms that I'd never heard spoken before. I don't think that was necessarily my parents' fault. I was intensely private as a kid, and I shuddered at discussing anything that felt overly vulnerable with anyone in my family unit. If my parents had ever tried to bring up sex, I definitely would have found a way to shut down the conversation. The *World Book Encyclopedia* provided most of the information I felt that I needed to know for the next seven or so years.

I felt a little jealous of my evangelical peers in my teen years and early twenties. They, like me, received instruction to be abstinent. From my perspective, though, they had much more compelling reasons to deny the desires of the flesh. While purity culture was indubitably psychically scarring for many, its inductees had the fire of Jesus' passion to outburn the fires of the flesh. The romance of being perfectly pure for an unknown knight in shining armor (from the female side of the coin, anyway) could also distract from the boredom of a romance-free life in the present.

The education I received, both tacit and explicit, could only reach so far into real life. For me and for many of my peers, there wasn't a script for sexual trauma. Were we still virgins when our "gifts" were taken without consent or when that consent was withdrawn? The limited knowledge I carried with me to college and beyond meant that I didn't even know what I was consenting to or refusing. Something of the teaching and silence we'd inherited had to be wrong.

My life took unexpected turns that didn't match the script I'd expected—while I won't go into too great of detail here, please know that the next few paragraphs discuss intimate partner violence. I dutifully waited until marriage, but when my first husband became violent early in our marriage, I began wanting a divorce. It took several years for me to realize my desire to end the marriage, as I struggled to know as a young and isolated woman how to leave the father of my children. Through a mixture of internalized blame for wanting to leave and the practical circumstance of being in graduate school with young children, I waited to leave until I had a stable job in my field. By that time we had two children together and another on the way.

I tell this part of my story not to give practical advice to anyone else. In my work as a chaplain, I always invite victims and survivors of abuse into safer lives for themselves and their children, if they have any. However, my experience was that leaving my marriage took a lot of time. When I finally found myself free, I was both confused and exhilarated, for a variety of reasons. When it came to sexuality, I faced the reality that the internalized narratives of purity culture fell short. The father of my three children wouldn't, presumably, be the only person I'd ever be with. I still felt young and alive, and I didn't want to live the next fifty or sixty years of my life in self-imposed celibacy. Maybe I was even a little angry that I had done all the "right" things (read: proper within the context of evangelically influenced purity culture) and still ended up in an awful and relatively brief marriage.

As a thirty-one-year-old single woman who'd known the agony of domestic violence and whose body had given birth to three children, my choices were bound to be different from those of the naive twenty-four-year-old who promised forever to a man who'd later physically harm her. After my divorce, I didn't have an underlying ethic for what sexual behavior should look like now. Clearly, my virginity was not a "gift" I could offer to a husband any longer, but, given my experiences in my first marriage, my non-virginity was the last thing on my mind.

I married again, this time to a man who came across as safe, responsible, and caring. I believed I was about to get a redo after my broken first experience of marriage. But within less than a year, I experienced a cycle of police calls, suicide attempts, and domestic violence episodes similar to those in my first marriage. I wasted no time in filing for divorce and securing a protection order. I'd already lived through one abusive marriage; I knew the over-quick heartbeat of panic, the feeling of trying to swallow the lump in my throat, and the blinding flash of hands that shattered reality. I refused to live through it again. I felt grim resolve to end the marriage to protect myself and my children, and with relatively little time to prepare for it emotionally or mentally, I represented myself and told my story to the civil court, police officers, the special victims unit, and the prosecutor's office. Through it all, I had never felt stronger, more clear in my intentions. Ultimately, my second ex-husband was incarcerated for his actions.

In the aftermath, I wondered, again, what was next, as I had no blueprint for what a Christian life was to look like in this situation. I still had not experienced the sacramental marriage relationship to which I aspire.

When I own my story, starting with the messages I received in childhood, I admit that as much as my family tried to distance itself from purity culture, we were influenced by it more deeply than we were ready to admit. And as much as we wanted to identify as progressive Christians, there wasn't a lot in my sexual formation that had the power to counteract the negative messages of purity culture. I'm guessing that I'm not alone in having messages from purity culture and secular culture on all sides but not a lot to help me to grow into a healthy, sexual adult.

I deserved a narrative for Christian sexuality that was more faithful and served me better. So many of my peers deserved better, too. We can't change the past, but we can shape our future and our children's future. As a parent, I've tried to take the best I experienced from my upbringing and heal the places I have been wounded—much as my parents did for me; much, I expect, as any parent tries to do for their children. I don't write this book to criticize my family or how they raised me, because there's much in my childhood that I still benefit from. I cringe to imagine how my children may reflect on *my* parenting when they're young adults, even despite my best efforts.

At the same time, I believe my kids need different stories, different ideas, as they grow into the people that God created them to be. They deserve to go into the world in strength and knowledge. I wrote 95 percent of this book while putting my kids to bed, lying down beside them with my laptop balanced on my knees, as two of them are still scared of falling asleep alone. I'm aware of how young and vulnerable they are right now, and also, how quickly the years leading up to adolescence will pass, and that one day, they'll make decisions and have relationships of their own. I hope that my daughters experience and learn from my fierce self-determination, both in my marriages and outside of them. I hope they learn that the value of marriage is not to fill an incompleteness, but to offer a partnership. I hope with all my heart that their choices honor themselves, their relationships, and ultimately God.

I want my children to know how deeply their bodies and the wholeness of their relationships matter to God. I want them to know the *eros* of the Divine who loved them first and knew them first. I want their hearts to be protected from those who would harm them. I want them to know that their sexual relationships are profoundly related to their faith. The best that evangelical Christianity has to offer, as far as sex goes.

But I also want them to know that their worth has nothing at all to do with their sexual relationships. That if they do choose intimacy, they aren't giving parts of themselves away—because sex doesn't confer ownership. That the Bible is about a whole lot of things, but dictating sexual behavior isn't the priority. That when others objectify them, it's not their fault, and it shouldn't be their problem. The best that progressive Christianity has to offer us, as far as sex goes.

What I want, all in all, is a whole-bodied biblical theology of sex that's worth sharing with my kids. I want it shameless and reverent. I want it solemn and joyful. I want it bold and vulnerable.

I haven't found what I'm looking for yet, so I decided to write it myself. If I could leave my children with one thing, it would be the capacity to live with themselves in their own bodies and relate to others in their own bodies, all while loving God above all.

It isn't always easy. I've felt the stress and tension of different ages and stages myself. While I haven't personally experienced *all* the stages, I accompany people as a chaplain and realize that my body and my children's bodies will have to find new ways to stretch and bend over time. Changing, all the time. Birthing, all the time. Leaking, all the time. Growing, all the time. Dying a little, even, all the time.

I want my children to love their bodies, created for pleasure and connection and life and death. I want them to know how to share their bodies, when the time and place is right for them, with reverence and love and boundaries and hope for a renewed world.

The following guiding principles orient me as I think about what I want to teach my children about sex.

Rather than primarily giving us a set of rules about sex, the Bible shows us how people navigate real life as imperfect yet beloved sexual beings. Jesus is much less interested in the details of our sex lives than in how we create relationships of justice and righteousness—in ways that include our sexual relationships. In the next few chapters, we'll look at how the scriptures talk about sex, in both the Old Testament and the New Testament.

What we do with our bodies is often a reflection of how we think about ourselves. And we need to think about ourselves as nothing less than *imago Dei*—the image of God. What we look like and how our bodies work is going to change over a lifetime. Our bodies will not always function like they do today—and for many of us, we live in the experience of disabled bodies now. Weight will change over a lifetime. Stretch marks may track across our bellies, hips, and thighs. Now, in my mid-thirties, I'm realizing that my blood sugar and cholesterol don't love me the way I wish they did when I go through stress-induced periods of unlimited pasta and ice cream eating. Our bodies will sicken at times, sometimes chronically, sometimes even attacking themselves (hello, autoimmune disease family! I see you!). Death will take each one of us.

And, in *all* of this, however we relate to the changes and varying states in our bodies, we are beloved of God, and we are imago Dei. How do we center this knowledge in our relationships? How do we live with ourselves and others as fully and uniquely beloved while also inviting each other to grow in and through our relationships?

I want my children to know, fully, who they are before they enter into intimate relationships with others, not because intimate activity involves giving away parts of themselves, but because our birthright identities come straight from God and should not be circumscribed or dictated by romantic partners. I want my kids to know that they are compassionate, brilliant, gorgeous, and fierce, and these are all ways that they, in their own ways, reflect the image of God. Sex and relationships do not give them their worth, and if that validation is what they look for through their connections with others, they'll be sadly disappointed.

Boundaries are good, healthy, and valuable. The boundaries that we choose should uphold our own values, honor where we are developmentally as people, and simply sit right with us. Boundaries can sometimes change over time. It's okay to set up one thing as a boundary and then change your mind later about where that line stands. Boundaries are traditionally a strong part of purity culture, though, and those kinds of boundaries—externally imposed, policed choices, uneven between two parties, especially men and women—aren't what I'm going for. Often, I've seen the boundaries of purity culture serve not young adults on the verge of sexual intimacy, but the families they represent, who want to control the sexuality of their children to preserve their own power and control. The mention of those sorts of boundaries gives me toe-curling discomfort. Yet I don't think that sexuality is, at its healthiest, a free-for-all either. The boundaries I'm talking about are not the ones about control, but those that we know in our own guts keep us safe and well.

Our nos are holy and sometimes prophetic. Our nos carve out the spaces where we can flourish, be well, and offer our gifts to a world that needs them. When we say no to something that we feel is wrong for us in relationship, we open ourselves up to the possibility of genuine connection in ways that are right for us. Sharing a boundary with somebody ought to be an opportunity to grow in knowledge and love of one another. Boundaries reflect what's happening inside of us. I believe that there is no such thing as genuine intimacy without boundaries. The goal of intimacy is not dissolution of selfhood, as if we're just amoebas who squish together and become a bigger amoeba, but two distinct selfhoods allowing each other to be known for who they really are—their yeses and their nos.

It's okay not to be okay as we're learning to navigate our sexuality. So many of us struggle to find health in our own conceptions of our sexuality, especially as we process what we've been taught and find new ways to be in the world. We need to normalize the fact that our sexual lives do not always go smoothly, and more often than not, we'll have one struggle or another during our lifetime. Even when we think that we have everything worked out for ourselves, these struggles may emerge in relationships when we're face-to-face with another person and have to confront what it means to be intimate with them.

Everyone can suffer from conditions that greatly impair sexual enjoyment. Lack of education, prior trauma, and harmful cultural attitudes can also play their own roles in making sex unpleasant, painful, and traumatic. To say that pleasure is God's longing for us through our sexuality is not to dismiss these experiences, but to encourage Christians to do better about educating people and facilitating access to treatment, including medical care, physical therapy, and psychotherapy.

Too many Christians have felt they had to walk through those challenges alone. There's often a wall of silence about these topics that we need to confront. The church doesn't talk enough about these things, but it definitely should talk about them more. God is with us in these struggles.

Healthy sexual relationships help us stretch our wings into the fullness of who God created us to be. Our selfhood is not up for grabs when we explore sexual relationships with others. Our selfhood, identity, and dignity were not conferred upon us through human hands, and human hands can't take them away. Too often, Christian discourse frames sexual activity as "giving parts of ourselves away." Women (usually women) cheat their future husbands if they explore sexuality outside of marriage commitment. A crumpled flower, a used tissue—whatever the crude analogy, the meaning is clear: if we share our bodies with anyone, we are becoming less ourselves and belong less to ourselves.

As a Christian mom, I repudiate the idea that my kids might think, ever, that somebody else can possess part of them. This idea, I believe, is rooted in some of the most problematic legacies of biblical interpretation out there. Having a sexual interaction with someone *does not mean* that they magically have an existential power over us.

Rather, the goal with relationships is that we become *more* ourselves as we explore them. We discover our own likes, dislikes, passions, and wounds as we interact in healthy and loving ways with other people. And we simultaneously help others grow and stretch and become their divinely created selves as well. We each give. We each receive. We each learn. We carry with us what we need for our journeys.

Pleasure and joy are often realizations of the best intentions that God has for our lives. This doesn't mean—at all—that our sexual activities should be indiscriminate. The deepest joy and pleasure come from right and healthy relationship. As Sheila Wray Gregoire and others have powerfully and poignantly pointed out, pleasure is part of God's design for sex, and it is a sin of purity culture that makes sex only about men's enjoyment to the exclusion and often exploitation of women.[2] The idea that pleasure is holy and good is not some newfangled invention of postmodernism. It's deeply biblical. The Song of Songs sensually illustrates pleasure for men *and* women, with a slant toward emphasizing the woman's experience. Make no mistake, there's enough in the Song of Songs to make the boldest among us blush.

* * *

Sometimes certain biblical texts tell stories and express ideas that are out of step with how we live in the world today. I often find meaning through the tension and conversation between all the different ways that God speaks to us in this world—while still acknowledging the Bible's unique, inspired role in telling the origins of the oldest and truest stories I know.

When it comes to sexuality, I think it can help us to move beyond seeing the Bible simply as a rule book. Scripture reflects many of the human dilemmas and challenges we face *and* it conveys much about the character of God. The eternal character of God reaches us even when the reflections of that character look different across cultures, times, and places. The goal of reading the Bible is not to reproduce what we see in it but to weave the story of God's transforming power through our own lives, in contexts far removed from anything that the biblical writers could have imagined.

There are a few areas where the movement of God today creates tension with the beliefs of the writers of Scripture when it comes to sexuality.

1. I think women have sexual desires too (well, duh!).
2. Relatedly, I think that consent is important.
3. I think all people ought to get a fair share of self-determination, without gender hierarchy.
4. I think all forms of sexual coercion are inexcusable, and I'm not really interested in the justification that women were considered men's property back then.

These are some pretty foundational ideas, and sometimes, core beliefs like these four lead me to grapple with the issue of sexuality in the Bible. Yet the tradition of those who have loved the Bible, for many centuries, has been to lovingly wrestle with it. After all, Jacob gets the name Israel by wrestling with an angel and refusing to let go until the angel blesses him. He becomes Israel, "he who wrestles with God" (see Genesis 32:22–32). The tradition of the rabbis and the church fathers calls us to be in deep and thoughtful conversation with Scripture to create the doctrines of the people of faith.

If those are my main areas of struggle with some of the biblical writers, I'm okay with that. And I invite you to sit in the discomfort of that divergence with me while also believing in a God who speaks to us through these ancient texts (among other things).

* * *

We need a better way forward for our communities—kids and adults alike—than what many of us were taught. I'm holding out the hope that my generation will heal ourselves as people and as parents and simply as caring adults who are part of kids' villages, and that we'll raise a generation of Christian youth who love the Bible and themselves as well. Who understand that applying Scripture to their lives means seeing it for what it is, a holy library of stories, poems, and prophecies of people who were imperfect, and who had to figure out how to live in their bodies and connect with others. Who know that through all the messy narratives and painful poems and poignant prophecies, God is there. And who see that as we try to figure out what it means to live in healthy and holy relationship with ourselves and one another, it gets messy and complicated, but God is there too.

The way forward involves addressing the harmful legacies of purity culture that hand over undue power to others in our relationships. It means dealing with the harmful legacies of progressive Christianity that fail to connect the dots between our sexualities and holiness. Carrying all our burdens and our gifts, taking them out of our rucksacks and seeing them for what they are, and choosing what to leave behind and what to repackage and share with others, we can move forward into health and wholeness and joy.

Perhaps, though, for all its complexity, what we need isn't more rules or standards or hedges to keep us out of sin. (Though staying out of sin is definitely something that I recommend, don't get me wrong.) Maybe we need to return to the heart of biblical teaching and then apply that teaching to sexuality, just like we would to any other area in our lives.

One time, Jesus was asked what the heart of biblical teaching was. The story goes like this:

> When the Pharisees heard that he had silenced the Sadducees, they gathered together, and one of them, an expert in the law, asked him a question to test him. "Teacher, which commandment in the law is the greatest?" He said to him, "'You shall love the Lord your God with all your heart and with all your soul and with all your mind.' This is the greatest and first commandment. And a second is like it: 'You shall love your neighbor as yourself.' On these two commandments hang all the Law and the Prophets." (Matthew 22:34–40)

Love God. Love neighbor. Love self. These three loves define a life that is lived faithfully, according to Jesus.

What if these three loves could define everything about our sexuality? What if, instead of drilling people about how they can fail in so many ways sexually (and otherwise), we could offer an invitation to sexual discernment that puts love of God, neighbor, and self at the center of everything? What if we could consider that the heart of biblical teaching regarding sexuality is this simple but transformative concept?

I'd like to find out. Please join me for the ride.

PART I

Sex Ed, Bible Style

1

The Old Testament

MORE THAN LAWS

As a parent, I love sharing stories with my children. They've picked up on this fact, and they'll often ask me to recount stories of their highlight reels as younger children ("Mom, tell me the story about the time I pooped in Cracker Barrel!"). When they're upset or uncertain, I've found that one of the ways I can comfort them is to tell them about my struggles as a younger person ("Hey, did I ever tell you about when my soccer coach made me be the goalie, and I never wanted to play soccer again?"). Even for little kids, there's something about knowing where we come from, how we've struggled and sometimes overcome, and how beloved we've been from the very beginning that grounds us.

And so, when we strive to understand ourselves as sexual beings, it might help to go back to the beginning. Because, in the canonical order of the biblical books right now, stories take up a lot of the first part of the Bible. And these are not just any stories. They are family stories. Stories of people who were born and died and prayed and struggled, so much like you and me. And I have to say that concerns about sex take up a lot of room in this material.

If we go back to the *very* beginning, we get Adam and Eve, as everybody knows. They basically get the best honeymoon suite of all time in Eden (though of course and unfortunately, that doesn't last) along with the command to be "fruitful and multiply," which sounds like an invitation to a good time if I've ever heard one! It's all "good," to quote God. Yet that's paired with the realization that loss of innocence and the striving to be equal to God in our personal agency, such as what happens when the first couple eats the apple, leads to suffering. Though Eve herself isn't cursed (Genesis 3:17–19 notes that the *ground* is cursed), the beautiful partnership of the garden is forever disrupted. It becomes tainted by inequality between the man and the woman. Pain (in childbirth) can result. And it's such a crying shame.

There's both joy and the potential pain in sex, right from the very beginning. The stories of the patriarchs that follow don't exactly simplify things. Sarah, desperate for a child, gives her enslaved maid Hagar to Abraham to impregnate, then is furiously jealous when Hagar's son Ishmael is a thriving child. Sarah fears that this could usurp her place in the family. Jacob sleeps with *the wrong sister* on his wedding night and then has to labor for another seven years to claim the bride he wanted (Laban might actually be the most obnoxious father-in-law ever). Judah denies his widowed daughter-in-law Tamar the support she's due, but his feigned righteousness is exposed as a sham when he sleeps with a prostitute who turns out to be Tamar herself.

Especially in agricultural societies, producing children meant ensuring family survival. So, obviously, a big focus of sex in the Old Testament is fertility and reproduction. Women in the Old Testament who aren't able to have children, permanently or temporarily, have a rough time, while those who bear children more easily receive cultural favor.

There are many stories of childless women or those who struggle with infertility in the Old Testament. Sex does not result in achieving their goal of children; their marriages are not fecund. This is such a big deal that it features prominently in the story of Abraham and Sarah. Their newly given covenant from God, when both are at an old age already, seems to contradict their circumstances of infertility. Later, angelic visitors confirm that a pregnancy will result from their sexual relationship. Sarah finds the pronouncement that she will conceive hilarious—as Genesis helpfully tells us, the two are no longer intimate. Sarah's laughter does not seem to me as much unfaithful as it does genuinely surprised and humorous, as the joke seems to be on her husband, who is no longer intimate with her.

> [The visitors] said to him, "Where is your wife Sarah?" And he said, "There, in the tent." Then one said, "I will surely return to you in due season, and your wife Sarah shall have a son." And Sarah was listening at the tent entrance behind him. Now Abraham and Sarah were old, advanced in age; it had ceased to be with Sarah after the manner of women. So Sarah laughed to herself, saying, "After I have grown old, and my husband is old, shall I be fruitful?" The LORD said to Abraham, "Why did Sarah laugh and say, 'Shall I indeed bear a child, now that I am old?' Is anything too wonderful for the LORD? At the set time I will return to you, in due season, and Sarah shall have a son." But Sarah denied, saying, "I did not

> laugh," for she was afraid. He said, "Yes, you did laugh." (Genesis 18:9–15)

Sarah's story of infertility to fertility is just one of many such stories in the Old Testament. God's provision through sexuality is ideally to produce children who will continue cultural legacies long beyond their parents' death.

Sex becomes a competition between the wives of Jacob, when Rachel is the preferred but less fertile wife and Leah is quite fertile but, in Jacob's eyes, less beautiful. Rachel's despair at her situation brings her to desperate measures: "When Rachel saw that she bore Jacob no children, she envied her sister, and she said to Jacob, 'Give me children, or I shall die!' Jacob became very angry with Rachel and said, 'Am I in the place of God, who has withheld from you the fruit of the womb?'" (Genesis 30:1–2). Ironically, it is not her infertility that will end her life, but her fertility, when she gives birth to her second son Benjamin. Like Sarah before her, Rachel's anxiety about having progeny leads her to take charge in a different way by having her husband procreate with her maid. Leah, too, later does the same.

Another (perhaps intended) consequence of the cultural focus on fertility is proscriptions against masturbation. Interestingly, masturbation becomes an issue of justice in Genesis 38. Onan is the younger brother of Er, who was "wicked in the sight of the Lord" and therefore died. As happened in ancient Israelite culture, Er's wife is given to Onan, the younger brother, to father children in Er's name to ensure his line will continue. Onan takes matters into his own hands, unwilling to sire children in his deceased brother's name.

> Judah said to [his son] Onan, "Go in to your brother's wife and perform the duty of a brother-in-law to her; raise

> up offspring for your brother." But since Onan knew that the offspring would not be his, he spilled his semen on the ground whenever he went in to his brother's wife, so that he would not give offspring to his brother. What he did was displeasing in the sight of the LORD, and he put him to death also. (Genesis 38:8–10)

This odd little story has a whole bunch of fallout. *Onanism* is now a disparaging term for masturbation in the English language. But this term, though effectively conveying disdain for masturbation, doesn't really capture what's wrong, from an ancient Israelite perspective, with masturbation in this scenario. First, Onan's masturbation denies Er what's due to him, which is to have children in his name to continue his family line. This is a big deal in ancient Israel. Without children, Er has no legacy. It's his younger brother's *duty* to impregnate Er's widow to ensure continuity.

But digging a little deeper, Onan's actions deny a widow what she's due as well. Er's widow Tamar is the one really left high and dry as a result of Er's erring. Without offspring from Er, Tamar is left without a family inheritance to sustain her. Failing to care for widows is one of the hallmarks of corrupt society in the Old Testament's books. Care for widows and orphans is a mandate of proper worship. See, for instance, Deuteronomy 14:28–29:

> Every third year you shall bring out the full tithe of your produce for that year and store it within your towns; the Levites, because they have no allotment or inheritance with you, as well as the resident aliens, the orphans, and the widows in your towns, may come and eat their fill so that the LORD your God may bless you in all the work that you undertake. (Deuteronomy 14:28–29)

Onan spurns this value by allowing his sperm to go other places than inside Tamar, because he should be creating an inheritance that will sustain her, and instead, he's just using his sexuality for pleasure, not for fruitfulness. For all these reasons, Onan loses his life; he, like his older brother Er, has done what is displeasing to God.

Probably for many of us, masturbation isn't inherently a big deal (though for some Christian groups, it is). However, regardless of where we stand on this issue, I love this little story about Onan because it reminds us that choices about our sexuality, no matter how trivial they might seem, can have big implications. Sexuality involves more than just our individual desires. What we do with our bodies affects not only ourselves, but our relationships with others, including our relationship with God. Sexuality, though deeply personal, is also communal in its implications. To claim that when we do whatever we want with our bodies we affect ourselves alone is simply not true in many cases. The ancient Israelites perhaps get this a lot better than twenty-first-century North Americans.

There are also a whole lot of rules governing sexual relations between people in the Torah, the first five books of the Hebrew Bible (what Christians refer to as the Old Testament). Virginity is prized as a way to guard the bloodlines of men who don't want to have to play guessing games about whose progeny a woman is carrying. A woman's value depreciates after she's had sex, so a "you break it, you buy it" mentality takes hold: if a man has sex with a woman before she is promised to him, he can expect to marry her and pay up. As Deuteronomy 22:28–29 says, "If a man meets a virgin who is not engaged and seizes her and lies with her, and they are discovered, the man who lay with her shall give fifty shekels of silver to the young woman's father, and she shall become his wife. Because he violated her, he shall not be permitted to divorce her as long as he lives."

In other words, having sex depreciates a woman's potential financial value for her father. The bride price he can expect to obtain is lower now that she has had sex. Virginity, in this specific context, is more financially rather than spiritually focused. It's a worthwhile endeavor to consider how the church's modern-day valuation of virginity is rooted in such an economic transaction. I don't mean that there's *no* spiritual value to virginity and abstinence, but we need to define it more carefully than simply claiming that it's obvious from all parts of the Bible! Probably, this idea of a daughter's virginity being tied up in a father and a husband's financial transaction disturbs many of us—and rightly so. This might feel too close to the tragedy of human trafficking for us to endorse it.

Sex is relational in part because we are to engage in it only with certain people. Every culture has limits as far as appropriate partners go; in North American culture, I've heard half-your-age-plus-seven as a pop psychology norm for the youngest person one should date, and it's obviously right to protect minors from predatory adults. The Torah articulates that sex is supposed to be human-to-human; bestiality is not permitted. And incest is strictly prohibited, too, as it is in cultures worldwide. Leviticus 20 gives several important prohibitions that set the cultural norms through which Israel are supposed to set themselves apart and live in just relationship with one another. Here is part of it:

> If a man commits adultery with the wife of his neighbor, both the adulterer and the adulteress shall be put to death. The man who lies with his father's wife has uncovered his father's nakedness; both of them shall be put to death; their

> bloodguilt is upon them. If a man lies with his daughter-in-law, both of them shall be put to death; they have committed perversion; their bloodguilt is upon them. If a man lies with a male as with a woman, both of them have committed an abomination; they shall be put to death; their bloodguilt is upon them. If a man takes a wife and her mother also, it is depravity; they shall be burned to death, both he and they, that there may be no depravity among you. If a man has sexual relations with an animal, he shall be put to death, and you shall kill the animal. If a woman approaches any animal and has sexual relations with it, you shall kill the woman and the animal; they shall be put to death; their bloodguilt is upon them. (Leviticus 20:10–16)

Sexual boundaries give definition to cultural identity, especially for a small and struggling people. The goal of these laws is holiness, or the status of being set apart from others. Whether or not it's historically true that other peoples were doing these kinds of acts that were abhorrent to the Levitical writer is irrelevant; rather, what matters is that they *thought* they were unique!

Mostly, the focus isn't really what makes for a healthy and holy sexual relationship between two people, but how sex serves to reinforce the cultural norms of the day. Problems arise when sexual activity falls outside traditional standards. The orientation in the sexual laws is toward creating or preserving a distinctive Israelite culture. This will be a culture in which the "seed" of God's people is separate and pure. When the Babylonians send many Judeans into exile while still others are allowed to remain in the land, things get messy. Decades after the exile began, the Persians allowed the exiles to return, whereupon they discovered that at least some of the people who stayed formed sexual relationships and marriages with those in other people groups.

The post-exilic books Ezra and Nehemiah deal with the breaches of tradition that took place when major cultural leaders were exiled and mixed marriages compromised the understood purity of the "holy seed." In short, there was holy hell to pay. Here's what happens in Ezra 9:

> The officials approached me [Ezra] and said, "The people of Israel, the priests, and the Levites have not separated themselves from the peoples of the lands with their abominations, from the Canaanites, the Hittites, the Perizzites, the Jebusites, the Ammonites, the Moabites, the Egyptians, and the Amorites. For they have taken some of their daughters as wives for themselves and for their sons. Thus the holy seed has mixed itself with the peoples of the lands, and in this faithlessness the officials and leaders have led the way." When I heard this, I tore my garment and my mantle and pulled hair from my head and beard and sat appalled. Then all who trembled at the words of the God of Israel because of the faithlessness of the returned exiles gathered around me while I sat appalled until the evening sacrifice. (Ezra 9:1–4)

Sex in ancient Israel and Judah involved not just coming together, but also coming together *with the right people* and separating from anybody who didn't fit that category. YHWH's people, traditionally, were supposed to maintain their cultural distinctiveness by sowing "holy seed" only in Judean fields—that is, women. But as cultural heritage often teaches us, it's hard to keep people apart who are very determined to get together. Even with harsh cultural sanctions, like Ezra and Nehemiah enforce by breaking up mixed marriages, we can imagine that idealistic leaders were hard-pressed to keep determined lovers apart.

The reality is that, even with these idealistic laws in place, human relationships often don't end at the edge of cultural acceptability. Relations between family members are a huge taboo—but Abraham passes off his wife Sarah as his sister when he goes into foreign territory! Intermarriage with people outside of the Israelite community is supposed to be a no-go—but Ruth, a Moabite woman, becomes folded into the family of Israel through marriage with Boaz. Nor does Ruth adhere to norms about male-female relations when she uncovers Boaz's "feet" on the threshing floor, outside of marriage! These are the instructions that Naomi, her mother-in-law, gives her to secure her place in Boaz's house:

> "My daughter, I need to seek some security for you, so that it may be well with you. Now here is our kinsman Boaz, with whose young women you have been working. See, he is winnowing barley tonight at the threshing floor. Now wash and anoint yourself, and put on your best clothes and go down to the threshing floor, but do not make yourself known to the man until he has finished eating and drinking. When he lies down, observe the place where he lies; then go and uncover his feet and lie down, and he will tell you what to do." [Ruth] said to her, "All that you say I will do." (Ruth 3:1–5)

The Bible contains enough euphemisms about feet that we have a pretty good idea that Ruth isn't just checking for Boaz's shoe size. This scene threatens scandal on multiple levels. Ruth is not married to Boaz, and she's also a Moabite. She also initiates sexual intimacy, which goes against the grain of the Old Testament of women being sexually receptive. Her actions, directed by Naomi, rupture the norms of sexuality.

Yet Ruth, despite these actions that could have made her a pariah, is none other than the great-grandmother of David. Prostitution is supposedly problematic, but Tamar, who disguises herself as a prostitute, is more righteous than Judah. And furthermore, going a bit further back into the history, the Canaanite prostitute Rahab is a heroine for her role in the Israelite conquest of Canaan. She protects the Hebrew spies who can slip into and out of her house because of its reputation as a brothel.

In the history of the Israelite monarchy, the sexual interactions of the kings and their nearest and dearest spell the ruin of dynasties. David rapes Bathsheba, cursing his monarchy. Too often, the story of David and Bathsheba is characterized only as adultery, without accounting for David's power and privilege as king. Unfortunately, the family's story of abuse continues, as abuse too often does. David's son Amnon follows in his footsteps by raping his half-sister Tamar, also David's child. Solomon, second child of the union forged after David has Bathsheba's husband killed, becomes king and marries many foreign (non-Jewish) wives, who corrupt the course of his reign. His flagrant sexuality distracts him from his primary duty of faithfulness: "Among his wives were seven hundred princesses and three hundred concubines, and his wives turned away his heart. For when Solomon was old, his wives turned away his heart after other gods, and his heart was not true to the Lord his God, as was the heart of his father David" (1 Kings 11:3–4). Following Solomon's weak end to his reign, his sons divide his kingdom, pointing to the end of independent Israelite rule.

In the writings of the Old Testament, sex is both something beautiful and alluring while also sometimes dangerously seductive. In Proverbs, which is structured as a series of instructions to young men, Folly is a sexy lady who lures good young men off the right track. Those who allow themselves to be seduced go into folly. In contrast, Wisdom is a chaste and virtuous woman who leads all who follow her on the right paths. Yet, properly channeled sexuality is viewed positively—Proverbs encourages young men to enjoy married sex:

> Let your fountain be blessed,
> and rejoice in the wife of your youth,
> a lovely deer, a graceful doe.
> May her breasts satisfy you at all times;
> may you be intoxicated always by her love.
> (Proverbs 5:18–19)

As strictly as Proverbs prohibits sexual dalliance, it encourages sexual joy within covenantal relationships.

Though these authors direct their admonitions exclusively to young men (because women weren't ordinarily thought of as having sexuality of their own), it's possible to extend their instructions to believers in general, as well. Sexuality *can* be used in ways that are dangerous and destructive. Sexuality *can* lead us further away from what God desires for our lives. But sexuality can also lead us toward God, one another, and ourselves. Sexuality can lead us to the fulfillment of our human desires in healthy ways.

In the books of the Prophets such as Jeremiah and Ezekiel, the emotional weightiness of sexuality is wielded to give a warning message to God's people (as well as sinful neighbors) who step out of line. The image of a loose, adulterous, or promiscuous woman is the pinnacle of sin to which idolaters are compared. Men and women alike, all who try to "marry" their worship to gods other than YHWH, are committing adultery. In graphic and disturbing language, the prophets describe both the indecent behavior involved as well as the often-sexualized punishments that these women—representing all sinful people—receive. These violent portraits of God's actions are likely disturbing to modern readers, and rightly so. In Ezekiel 16 and 23, the sisters Oholah and Oholibah represent Israel and Judah, who have "fornicated" with foreign peoples and their gods, their sexual acts symbolizing disloyalty to YHWH. They have acted the part of "prostitutes," who, in the understanding of the writers, cheapen sexual favors by peddling them. First, Ezekiel gives examples of the types of acts that the "sinful" sisters are engaging in. Here's Ezekiel's description of the activities of Oholah:

> She bestowed her sexual favors upon them, the choicest men of Assyria all of them, and she defiled herself with all the idols of everyone for whom she lusted. She did not give up her prostitutions that she had practiced since Egypt, for in her youth men had lain with her and fondled her virgin bosom and poured out their lust upon her. (Ezekiel 23:7–8)

Then comes the punishment:

> Therefore I delivered her into the hands of her lovers, into the hands of the Assyrians, for whom she lusted. These uncovered her nakedness; they seized her sons and her daughters, and they killed her with the sword. Judgment was executed upon her, and she became a byword among women. (Ezekiel 23:9–10)

Sexual misbehavior is followed by sexualized terrorism, which may not reassure us about God or even, perhaps, about the end results of engaging in sex at all! Ezekiel proposes a Dantesque punishment based on what one chooses in excess in life. In the world of the text, Oholah and Oholibah have chosen sexual infidelity to God, so God punishes them by oversaturating them with unwanted sexual experiences, exposing their nakedness to their lovers. It's hard not to visualize a gang rape with this kind of language being used.

No one deserves to be sexually abused, regardless of sexual or any kind of sin. A victim's sin is irrelevant to whether abuse is wrong, and victims have done nothing to deserve their treatment. As readers of biblical texts who are rightly sensitized to issues of abuse from movements like #MeToo and their own experiences, reading these texts is painful, jarring, and even traumatic. Yet it's interesting that the intended audience of these writings—namely a group of elite men—are compared to female sex workers, often on the margins of society. The prophets' language about sex, however disturbing, discomfits elites of the day who may be self-righteous about their own morality. *Real* morality involves a lot more than simply following a set of rules.

In the Song of Songs, which I'll discuss in a lot more detail later, sexuality is openly celebrated. The poetic book is open about the desires and pleasures that humans experience, and it beautifully alternates between a man and woman sharing about their experience. The concern of marriage and legal exchanges between the parents of the bride and the groom aren't central at all; if anything, the people trying to regulate the couple's sexual ecstasy are the bad guys!

The Hebrew Bible seems to offer an expansive portrait of what sexuality in our world looks like, with a bit of fantasy, realism, practicality, regulation, and ecstasy all thrown in. If someone were to ask me, "What does the Hebrew Bible say about sex?," I'd be hard-pressed to give a short answer. What I could say, though, is that rather than giving a simple portrait of idealized sexuality, it portrays what sexuality is within the messiness of our reality.

Sexuality is complicated. It's about people coming together to share bodies and emotions, but it's also about the places we come from—our families, our cultural backgrounds, and our faith. It's about doing what makes sense to create social harmony and cohesion, but it's also about passion and love. It's deeply emotional, but it also involves very pragmatic considerations. In short, there's a lot to think about.

And I think that we need the complicated stories of Scripture to help guide us through. We need stories and songs of people who struggled in their lives, sometimes made awful decisions about how to interact with others, failed to love their bodies like God does, yet also enjoyed each other in beautiful moments of ecstasy. And while there are "rules" to be sure, what most remains in my mind and heart is the stories. Knowing that there were other people like me who were human and imperfect and beloved.

I think it's funny that in church, we're often so reluctant to expose our young people to the sexually tinged parts of Scripture. As if the scandal will rub off on them and, like Tamar, they'll hang out on the side of the road to seduce their fathers-in-law, or, like Absalom, lust after their sister-in-law. Scripture mirrors reality because it comes from reality, from this messy, broken, and beautiful world that God loves and calls his own. There's nothing in Scripture that should be especially shocking to us, because we live in the same world that Scripture came from. There are differences in time and place, obviously, but in essence, our world is the same. People fall in love and in lust. They seek out companionship and affection, sometimes in all the wrong places.

What are we so afraid our young people will see or hear from Scripture that they haven't seen or heard or will see or hear from somewhere else in their lives? Honestly, I don't think

Scripture represents anything, as awful and gory and glorious (gor-ious?) as it is, that isn't true to the world we live in. And this is not just a "if they're not hearing it here, they'll hear it somewhere else" situation. What better place than the community of God's people to hear about these types of scenarios in the redemption story of the world? The messiest and most confusing and most sacred and most beautiful moments of our embodied experience are included in the story of Scripture, the story of how God redeems and sanctifies our humanity.

As humans, we can be pretty good at compartmentalization. We see this in the garden of Eden, where Adam and Eve squander their perfect relationship with God and each other, all for the sake of becoming like God, and then try to hide and lie about it. When YHWH is walking in the garden, Adam tries to avoid the fact that God already knows what's amiss in their relationship. Hiding is silly; God knows everything, anyway. God is intimately involved in every part of our lives, including, well, the intimate parts.

So to pretend that we're making our kids and ourselves more holy by not taking an honest look at the messier and steamier and more graphic parts of Scripture because those parts are separated from God isn't just impossible compartmentalization, it's also downright heretical. God is in the midst of all the gritty parts of being human. Our choice and responsibility must be to integrate these parts of ourselves into our faith lives, much as the Hebrew Bible weaves everything together into its narrative testimony of faith. God is already well aware of our innermost thoughts, experiences, and desires, and overlooking them shuns a part of ourselves that matters deeply to God.

I am grateful for the witness of our sacred texts that sexuality is part of how God meets us and one of the aspects of our lives that God intends to renew and transform in the making of all things new. After all, God's own relationship to humanity is characterized as that of a lover or spouse; the passion of human-to-human relationships is only a faint mirroring of God's own passion for us. Aside from the Song of Songs, one of the loveliest examples of this image is in the later parts of the prophetic book of Isaiah:

> For Zion's sake I will not keep silent,
>   and for Jerusalem's sake I will not rest,
> until her vindication shines out like the dawn
>   and her salvation like a burning torch.
> The nations shall see your vindication
>   and all the kings your glory,
> and you shall be called by a new name
>   that the mouth of the LORD will give.
> You shall be a beautiful crown in the hand of the LORD
>   and a royal diadem in the hand of your God.
> You shall no more be termed Forsaken,
>   and your land shall no more be termed Desolate,
> but you shall be called My Delight Is in Her
>   and your land Married,
> for the Lord delights in you,
>   and your land shall be married.
> For as a young man marries a young woman,
>   so shall your builder marry you,
> and as the bridegroom rejoices over the bride,
>   so shall your God rejoice over you. (Isaiah 62:1–5)

For Isaiah, speaking to a people dispossessed and seemingly abandoned, the best image to indicate God's active, continued choosing of Israel was that of a wedding ceremony. God is the rebuilder of the ruined Jerusalem, but God is also the bridegroom who delights in the beauty of the bride, Zion. Just as a marriage ceremony often involves a change of names, more typically on the part of the woman, the dazzling bride, God's own city, puts aside old names of shame—Forsaken and Desolate—and takes on names related to the Lord's relationship with her. In holy union with God, the proper name for Jerusalem is "My Delight Is In Her" and her land is "Married." The history of pain that predates this marriage no longer defines her; rather, Zion is defined by the identity that God gives her as spouse. God celebrates the beauty of the bride as he vindicates her, holding her as crown and diadem.

I wish that the many of us who struggle with our identity, especially concerning the hurt and brokenness we experience in all kinds of relationships, could hear this passage as spoken from God straight to us. As we contend for our identities and experiences to be acknowledged, God is our advocate; for our sake, as for Jerusalem, God will not keep silent. God regards each of us, part of the holy people he has called to himself, as a work of art like a crown or diadem in his hands. In baptism, we also join the life of God in Christ and step into our identity as a member of God's household. The intimacy that we can experience with God is deeper than what we can have in any human relationship. In the same way that marriage was traditionally structured in the ancient world, this relationship happens at the initiative of Christ the bridegroom. We are sought out, chosen, and adored before we even know that we have the choice to respond to God. God *desires* each of us, claims us for his own.

Perhaps this way of thinking about God's tender and passionate pursuit of us comes as a bit of a surprise to those of us Christians who have grown up relatively alienated from the Old Testament. I know that passages like Isaiah 62 weren't part of my own Christian upbringing. The multidimensional portrait of God found in the Old Testament teaches us that the passion of human emotions is nothing compared to that of God's. At times, the vivid and graphic imagery may threaten to drive us away, as God rails against human injustice, but God's passionate love undergirds every other expression of emotion. The Jesus who flips over tables in the temple is the incarnation of the God whose love burns for all people.

I think that the sexual choices we regret so often come from the fear that we are not enough. Like Adam and Eve in the garden of Eden, who have it all but are hoodwinked into thinking they need to be like gods, we often choose from a feeling of inadequacy. We reach for a relationship or a sexual activity because we feel like we need it to validate us, as if a relationship could ever really provide the reassurance that we are enough. We engage in sexual activities indiscriminately or even against our own better judgment because it feels like, even for a moment, sex will complete us.

But sex, as beautiful and empowering and wonderful as it can be in the right context, doesn't do those things for us. Sex is powerful, but it doesn't have the power to transmute an identity to heal us. It can't change an identity steeped in pain and betrayal to one in love.

The deep love and passion that God harbors for us—so profound that the closest thing we can compare it to is physical passion—needs to be at the root of all our understandings of romantic passion. God loves us first. God claims us first. Amid all the messiness and pain and struggle of the Old Testament, God is there speaking to us, teaching us from the depths of human experience. God is there inviting us into the fullness of life.

2

Jesus and the Gospels

A LOVE THAT EMBRACES

For all that the Old Testament paints a complicated portrait of sex, the New Testament gets more credit in setting the sexual norms for Christianity today. That makes sense. For many Christians, the New Testament is the flowering and fulfillment of the Old Testament. Jesus is the full bloom of the seeds sown in the Old Testament. So he and his apostolic buddies would be the real authorities on sex, right?

Well, kind of. The early church has a good number of teachings on sexuality, but Jesus's instructions on sexual behavior are sparse. Jesus and his earliest followers had other things on their minds than sex and marriage for the most part, but as the time lengthened since Jesus' life and the early church got set up, it was important to figure out how, exactly, sexuality figured in.

The progressive Christians I grew up with often said that Jesus doesn't talk a lot about sexuality. By making this point, progressive Christians hope to liberate believers from a rules-based theology that further marginalizes vulnerable people. In a way, I think they're right, and in another way, I think they're very wrong. Jesus doesn't dole out a list of commandments about sexuality, but the way his stories are told should guide us as we live out our God-given sexuality. The stories shared by the gospel writers about Jesus point us toward graciousness, humility, and love in our interactions with others when it comes to sex. It's not simply Jesus' *words* that tell us what we need to learn about sexuality from him, but also his whole life.

Jesus' virgin birth frames the New Testament's insights on sexuality. Jesus is conceived without sex involved. Matthew, following the genealogy, tells the annunciation story, of how Mary consents to bear God into the world. A human woman, she is nevertheless unique in the role that she plays to miraculously conceive a child by the Holy Spirit. She says a surprising yes to God that models how all believers can hope to answer yes to the divine calling on our lives.

The virgin birth is regarded differently across Christian groups. Growing up as a liberal Protestant, I attended a lecture by John Dominic Crossan, a famous historical Jesus scholar, when I was thirteen or fourteen (remember the obscure homeschooling) where I heard that, most likely, Jesus was the illegitimate son of a Roman soldier.[1] Since then, I've encountered Christians across the entire spectrum of belief about Jesus' divinity, from Mennonites who respect Mary and regard her as a courageous prophet who models faithfulness and discipleship to Catholics who believe that Mary was prepared to be special from her *own* immaculate conception (she herself was born without sin) and miraculously conceived Jesus without human involvement, and whose unequaled relationship to Jesus makes her an intercessor for the church.

Regardless of how Christians theologically understand Mary today, living in first-century Palestine, Mary would have faced certain stigma for her pregnancy. Her yes to God is even more radical because she would have *appeared* to be a woman who was sexually promiscuous. Her chastity is apparent through the conversation with the angel:

> The angel Gabriel was sent by God to a town in Galilee called Nazareth, to a virgin engaged to a man whose name was Joseph, of the house of David. The virgin's name was Mary. And he came to her and said, "Greetings, favored one! The Lord is with you." But she was much perplexed by his words and pondered what sort of greeting this might be. The angel said to her, "Do not be afraid, Mary, for you have found favor with God. And now, you will conceive in your womb and bear a son, and you will name him Jesus. He will be great and will be called the Son of the Most High, and the Lord God will give to him the throne of his ancestor David. He will reign over the house of Jacob forever, and of his kingdom there will be no end." Mary said to the angel, "How can this be, since I am a virgin?" The angel said to her, "The Holy Spirit will come upon you, and the power of the Most High will overshadow you; therefore the child to be born will be holy; he will be called Son of God. And now, your relative Elizabeth in her old age has also conceived a son, and this is the sixth month for her who was said to be barren. For nothing will be impossible with God." Then Mary said, "Here am I, the servant of the Lord; let it be with me according to your word." Then the angel departed from her. (Luke 1:26–38)

Sliding to another gospel narrative, Matthew tells about Jesus' beginnings through the lens of Isaiah 7:14, which, as commonly translated by Christians, reads, "Behold, a virgin will conceive and bear a son" (NIV). In Hebrew, the word *betulah*, translated commonly as "virgin," literally just means "young woman," and the Isaiah text refers to the coming of King Hezekiah to deliver Israel from the Assyrians. In the Septuagint, the Greek translation of the Hebrew Bible, *betulah* in Hebrew becomes *parthenos* (virgin), which is what Matthew is drawing upon. In Christian theology, Mary's virginity becomes important because it emphasizes how Jesus will be different—fully divine and fully human—even as he enters the messy world of human sin and suffering.

This idea of Mary being a virgin—and therefore able to bear the unique Son of God—has influenced Christian culture by making virginity before marriage a value of the faithful as well. Mary is someone to revere and emulate, regardless of denominational affiliation. But the point of Mary is not *mainly* her virginity in and of itself, though many Christians do believe that the unique story of the annunciation sets the stage for Jesus' extraordinary life. And if Mary's example is used to harm and shame God's children who are no longer virgins, well, that seems antithetical to the message of a good, nurturing, and loving parent.

Mary's story might lead us in a polar opposite direction, of recognizing the totality of obedience to God, even when that path might lead us in directions that might be scorned and condemned by society. Mary's yes to God meant that she experienced a pregnancy out of wedlock, a situation severe enough to potentially put her life in danger at maximum and, at minimum, to ensure a broken engagement to her fiancé Joseph. Matthew 1:18–25 tells the story of how Joseph's dream (connecting him to the *other* Joseph, from the book of Genesis, who was also a dreamer) spared Mary the penalty of even private rejection:

> When his mother Mary had been engaged to Joseph, but before they lived together, she was found to be pregnant by the Holy Spirit. Her husband Joseph, being a righteous man and unwilling to expose her to public disgrace, planned to divorce her quietly. But just when he had resolved to do this, an angel of the Lord appeared to him in a dream and said, "Joseph, son of David, do not be afraid to take Mary as your wife, for the child conceived in her is from the Holy Spirit. She will bear a son, and you are to name him Jesus, for he will save his people from their sins." All this took place to fulfill what had been spoken by the Lord through the prophet:
>
> "Look, the virgin shall become pregnant and give birth to a son,
> and they shall name him Emmanuel,"
>
> which means, "God is with us." When Joseph awoke from sleep, he did as the angel of the Lord commanded him; he took her as his wife but had no marital relations with her until she had given birth to a son, and he named him Jesus. (Matthew 1:18–25)

Joseph is one of my favorite biblical characters. Faced with what looks from the outside like an emasculating situation of heartbreak in which another man has impregnated his fiancée, he ends up trusting Mary and the word of God given to him, and he *believes the account of events that Mary tells about her own experience*. How often must women, whether in relationships, medical offices, or courts, face an unsympathetic audience of others, especially men, who do not believe what women are reporting about their own experiences? Far too often, in my opinion. Joseph is different. Joseph has every right to walk away or worse, but his response is, like Mary's, obedience to God. Joseph becomes protector, advocate, and provider for this vulnerable woman and unborn child. According to some Christian traditions such as Catholicism, he even remains chaste to protect the sanctity of his spouse, the *theotokos* (God-bearer).

Still, in the gospel of Luke, Mary's pregnancy is a source of extreme vulnerability, even though and especially because it comes from God. Mary leaves her town to the rural country to visit her cousin Elizabeth. For a pregnant woman, this trip must not have been easy. Perhaps she left simply to escape the shame of the unforgiving public eye. But it is also possible that Mary left for her own safety. In Deuteronomy, women who are raped in the city can face capital punishment—in the city, a woman being raped could hypothetically cry out for help, but in the country, women in compromising situations who cry out for help may not be heard (Deuteronomy 22). Perhaps Mary's actions are guided by her fears about this law. Mary goes to a country region to meet Elizabeth, so that when her pregnancy is detected, she cannot be accused and punished for sex with another man.

Through Mary's story, the gospel writers give us a respect for the idiosyncrasy of people's stories when it comes to sexuality. Our journeys, even when lived out within obedience to God's will, can look bizarre or disreputable from the outside. Just as Joseph was called upon by God to believe Mary, to hear her story, and to accept her experiences, we too are called to accompany people along their God-given paths rather than condemn them.

Matthew introduces Jesus to us through a genealogy, as does Luke, though they are not one-for-one matches. Matthew takes pains to show the history of Jesus' descent, to link him to the ancestral stories of faith. I know that I, for one, am tempted to let my eyes glaze over when we enter genealogy territory in Scripture, but this one is especially important for Christians. There's plenty else to say about the genealogy of Jesus here, but one important feature is that it includes five women: Tamar, Rahab, Bathsheba, Ruth, and Mary. What's extraordinary about all these women—four of them from the Old Testament and one of them from the New Testament—is that all of their stories involve something sexually scandalous.

Tamar seduced her father-in-law to reclaim her due and family line.

Rahab was a prostitute trying to navigate between two cultures.

Bathsheba's offspring joined the family tree through David's rape.

Ruth was a Moabite woman who boldly took sexual initiative to secure a future.

And Mary, bless her, was a young woman who could easily have been considered an adulteress after she became pregnant by the Holy Spirit.

Jesus' genealogy puts it all out there, that Jesus is from survivors of a harsh and hostile world such as these women, in a powerful opening statement about his life and ministry. Jesus breaks into the story of humankind not by seclusion from its messy realities, not by exclusion of those who don't conform to social norms, but by joining it in solidarity. The New Testament writers assume the presence and importance of people, especially of women, whose life stories didn't match the norm, without whom the family lineage of Jesus would be incomplete.

As far as we know from the gospel accounts, Jesus was a single, celibate man. Though the fan fiction of his life often imagines him as a married person (and to be fair, marriage would have been the norm for a Jewish rabbi of his time), we see Jesus also adopting a lifestyle that involved frequent travel from place to place, and a life that was wholly oriented toward his mission of announcing the kingdom. Could Jesus have been married? Sure, he *could* have been, if that was God's desire for him.

After all, the New Testament takes care to show us that Jesus experienced the fullness of human life, even including temptations. The book of Hebrews refers to Jesus' temptations as pervasive like those of humans:

> Since, then, we have a great high priest who has passed through the heavens, Jesus, the Son of God, let us hold fast to our confession. For we do not have a high priest who is unable to sympathize with our weaknesses, but we have one who in every respect has been tested as we are, yet without sin. Let us therefore approach the throne of grace with boldness, so that we may receive mercy and find grace to help in time of need. (Hebrews 4:14–16)

The burning question is: did Jesus also experience sexual temptations, or was he so perfect as the Son of God that he could not experience these as well? If we take Hebrews seriously, we might conclude that yes, Jesus did in fact experience sexual temptation. If Jesus can truly "sympathize with our weaknesses," then he knew also the sexual weaknesses that many of us experience.

But the assumption that Jesus had to have been married can also reflect a bias within the church toward married people. What if Jesus' singleness and celibacy reflects a valid and fulfilling lifestyle of mission not just for Jesus, but for other single people in the church? What if married life isn't the only way to fulfillment?

As many Christian religious orders and ascetics have recognized, singleness can allow a person to focus fixedly on God without the obligations of a spouse and children to demand (rightfully) one's time. For too long, churches have idolized marriage as the singular choice for people in adulthood to live a complete life. Perhaps it's time to refocus ourselves on Jesus' singleness to remind ourselves that it can be and is enough for many people to live in committed relationship fully with God, who is spouse and counselor to each of us. The "normal" path through adulthood does not need to be defined by marriage or sexual relationships to be free, full, and joyful. Single people can be witnesses to the church of a lifestyle given wholly to the love and pursuit of God and joyful service to the community.

Jesus has a lot of things to say about a variety of topics, but sex isn't high on his list by any standard. Interestingly, four stories about him that come closest involve interactions with women. It seems Jesus, when presented the opportunity to talk *about* women or *to* women, prefers the latter. Their lives, their stories, their brokenness, matter to Jesus, more than any custom of his day or ours. Jesus' engagement with sexual topics emerges through his compassionate relationships with women.

First, let's turn to the woman caught in adultery: A woman condemned for her sexual sin is dragged before Jesus. The gospel of John tells the story with an eye to the drama and the motives of all the characters:

> Early in the morning [Jesus] came again to the temple. All the people came to him, and he sat down and began to teach them. The scribes and the Pharisees brought a woman who had been caught in adultery, and, making her stand before all of them, they said to him, "Teacher, this woman

> was caught in the very act of committing adultery. Now in the law Moses commanded us to stone such women. Now what do you say?" (John 8:2–5)

The teachers want to see whether Jesus will follow the law and demand her death. She is a woman they want to talk *about* with Jesus. She's an object to be shamed and scorned, not a human to be understood. She's just a pawn in their game to destroy Jesus by showing that he won't obey tradition. This tidbit catches my attention, because the leaders seem to *know already* that Jesus will show grace to the woman. This will be their "gotcha" moment when they catch him red-handed in an unsanctioned act of mercy. Their prediction that they can get Jesus this way tells me that there were many other interactions where Jesus embodied the full spirit of the Law by extending grace and mercy to sinners, the lowliest of the low, like this woman.

Though this story appears in a different gospel account from those that announce Jesus' birth, I wonder if Jesus looked at this poor woman, exposed, and thought of his own mother. Mary, too, could have been accused of adultery, for she was found to be pregnant by an unknown father while engaged to Joseph. She, too, could have faced death by stoning. At minimum, she could have been publicly shamed by Joseph and sent away, had Joseph not resolved to send her away quietly and then, directed by divine intervention, agreed to keep her as his wife.

I think that Jesus looked at this woman as the son of Mary, and had mercy, the way his mother too was spared. His address to her, "Woman," matches that to his own mother, earlier in John at the wedding at Cana: "Woman, what concern is that to me and to you?" (John 2:4). He intervenes because he is God, yes, full of both mercy and justice, but on a human level, the woman's plight appeals to his filial piety. His human upbringing taught him that things can often not be what they seem, that a woman accused without a man in sight may just be a woman in trouble rather than sin.

But truthfully, the leaders aren't really following the law, either. They're inconsistent in its application because not just the woman, but the man, too, is supposed to be stoned. Leviticus 20:10–12 and Deuteronomy 22:22–24 specify that *both* guilty parties are to be put to death, not just the woman. This exposed women surely did not commit adultery alone. Yet for some strange reason (read: patriarchy), the man is spared this ordeal of public humiliation while the woman must endure it.

Jesus tacitly declines to respond right away to the case brought before him. Beautifully, he kneels down and writes something on the ground with his finger (John 8:6). We don't know what Jesus writes. Is it a list of commandments? A symbol? But what becomes apparent to me is the contrast in stature between Jesus and all others in the scene. Jesus is originally *sitting*, as a rabbi was expected to, while those he engaged in teaching stood. He's in a place of honor. The woman is brought to *stand* before him. But Jesus ultimately *kneels*. He makes himself lower than this woman accused of a deplorable sin.

As a parent and a chaplain, I've learned that body positioning matters. Towering over my child in a moment of anger or meltdown (theirs or mine) really isn't helpful. Standing far above a person I'm trying to speak to in a pastoral way reinforces the power difference between them and me. Usually, it helps to be on or below people's level when you're trying to restore calm and agency to them.

And I think this is what Jesus is doing here. He lowers himself to below the woman's level to teach the crowd—and her—what really matters.

Incidentally, I think that the woman's response to Jesus changes her far more than a harsh rebuke ever could have. I suspect she well knows what she's done, if she's indeed guilty of the adultery of which they accuse her. How could she not be burning in shame and self-rebuke at this moment of confrontation?

On the door of a confessional at a historic Catholic church in my neighborhood, a rendering of this story covers several feet of space. It's perfect for this context, because confession in Christian churches is meant to expose the most painful aspects of our distance from God—not to the world, as the religious leaders try to flaunt so cruelly, nor to God, for God already knows, but to ourselves. Humbling ourselves with the reality of our shortcomings is the only way that we can truly find healing in God's mercy. Deepening our self-hatred through self-flagellation, or receiving the judgment of our community around us, isn't really what causes us to grow. It's knowing how far from the mark we fall, yet receiving the welcome of a Savior who ministers to the lost.

And that's why Jesus' response to the woman is so powerful. Down below her level, his posture will later be reflected in his washing of the feet at the Last Supper before his arrest in the garden of Gethsemane: "Jesus, knowing that the Father had given all things into his hands and that he had come from God and was going to God, got up from supper, took off his outer robe, and tied a towel around himself. Then he poured water into a basin and began to wash the disciples' feet and to wipe them with the towel that was tied around him" (John 13:3–5). Kneeling, this gesture of humility, where the respected teacher gets lower than the (presumed) lowest sinner in the room, shakes everything up. Just like the hubbub and offense generated when sports players kneel during the national anthem in protest of the abuse of Black Americans, when Jesus kneels, he too causes offense by dismantling systems of shame that threaten to keep sinners away from a God who welcomes all home.

Jesus, kneeling, interrupts the gradient of power that places the woman at the bottom, putting himself there instead. He invites his audience, who is watching his every move, to identify with the woman instead of pitting themselves against her. His response, cleverly phrased, in its most surface-level interpretation, seems to invite the legally imposed penalty. He breaks his humble gesture of kneeling only to redirect those who would be ready to kill the woman for her sins: "When they kept on questioning him, he straightened up and said to them, 'Let anyone among you who is without sin be the first to throw a stone at her.' And once again he bent down and wrote on the ground" (John 8:7–8).

Growing up, one of the Scripture verses planted in my mind was Romans 3:23, which I memorized as "All have sinned and all fall short of the glory of God." We aren't perfect people, and we often find ourselves straying from the paths God has for us. Our condemnation, short of the grace of God made known in Christ, is sure. Yet this message that we are *all* in the place of condemnation, and therefore, that nobody ought to throw stones at anyone, least of all the shamed woman, is one that drives people away. The people gathered to condemn the woman go away one by one, "beginning with the elders," until only Jesus and the woman remain. (One of my favorite things to look for in the Gospels is what drives people away from Jesus. On this occasion, his *mercy* is offensive. Might be just me, but it seems like Jesus did a much better job scaring off followers with the strength of his teachings than attracting them. It's a hard road to the cross, after all.)

Jesus treats us, like the woman, as subjects, not objects. We are the ones he meets with love and grace. He looks at us with eyes of love and speaks to us directly:

> Jesus straightened up and said to her, "Woman, where are they? Has no one condemned you?" She said, "No one, sir." And Jesus said, "Neither do I condemn you. Go your way, and from now on do not sin again." (John 8:10–11)

Jesus' posture shifts again so they can address each other as companions (though we know that Jesus is the Son of God and no one's equal, and there were differences of power between men and women in Jesus' culture). Jesus desires to engage the woman as a human, an individual with her own thoughts about and experience of her situation. Instead of interpreting the situation *for* her, he asks her, "Where are they? Has no one condemned you?" She is empowered to declare for herself that she is no longer facing condemnation. Jesus' own mercy comes after her recognition that she faces condemnation from no other person. She is right to perceive that she has exited the realm of condemnation and entered into the reign of grace.

Jesus, the only one with the power to condemn anyone, condemns no one. He gives her the opportunity for a fresh start, even after sin that could define anyone's life. The exoneration from the imminent threat of death isn't a free-for-all; as Paul says, faced with grace, our impetus to live a life of righteousness is all the greater: "What then are we to say? Should we continue in sin in order that grace may increase? By no means! How can we who died to sin go on living in it?" (Romans 6:1–2).

Receiving grace doesn't make us less motivated to live in newness of life with God—it makes us all the more eager for it. Like a child who makes a grave error and hurts their relationship with a parent and then is welcomed home with a loving embrace (serious prodigal son vibes here), receiving grace folds us back into the household with more passion and commitment. We don't want to damage a relationship in which someone has shown us such love. And so I'm willing to bet that this encounter with Jesus changed the woman. I don't think she went back to the man with whom she had been (supposedly) caught in adultery. Receiving light, she walked in light (John 8:12).

There are innumerable ways that we can fall short of God's vision for us in our sexuality. We can fail to honor one another as created in the image of God and as inherently valuable people. When we respond to news of people committing what we consider sexual sins, our temptation is to let the stigma of what they've done attach to them and define them. We are to always treat people as people: created and loved by God.

If Jesus has any straightforward lessons to teach us about sexuality, then, it may be that we are in no position to declare anyone outside of God's mercy and justice. Otherwise, we might as well be stoning ourselves, because we too are guilty.

Please note: *circumstances of sexual abuse dictate careful and responsible decisions about community life.* God loves sex offenders, no question about it. My experiences as a chaplain have included work with people convicted of sex offenses, and this has shaped me in many ways. These sins do not define their souls before God. But these types of offenses are violent or coercive and should lead communities to make smart choices about protecting others. Grace and safety are not at odds. But reintegration into community as if nothing happened isn't possible or even remotely responsible. Grace means that offenders can be assured of love and care and inclusion insofar as all vulnerable people are protected. Grace does not mean denial of the sin (and Jesus' mercy doesn't do that, either!).

A lot of times, people say, "I'm not judging you" when somebody offers a vulnerable story of their sexual past. But those words usually belie the vulnerable person's real experience of being judged. It's not enough to *say* that we're not judging someone, or to say we "hate the sin, not the sinner," when a vulnerable person is left outside our tables and pews. Jesus is in our midst, kneeling at our feet, writing on the ground, saying, "Whoever is without sin, throw the first stone." Jesus puts those who would judge to shame, leading us to leave, wordless, when he speaks directly to the one we'd cast stones at.

So wherever we draw lines, wherever we throw stones, we can be assured that Jesus is on the other side of them, welcoming sinners (like us), drawing people home to the Father, and redeeming their lives. This does not mean that Jesus invites people to persist in sin, but rather that the encounter he mediates with God empowers them to live righteous lives.

I'm aware that different readers will draw lines in different places; for some, lines around extramarital sex; for others, lines around LGBTQ identity or relationships; for still others, the correctness of allowing minors to pursue gender-redefining procedures. And what we teach our children about each of these concerns likely matters to each of us. While I have opinions on each of these topics, it's less important to share my views than to encourage parents to have genuine conversations with their kids about sexuality in ways that center the gospel. It's not that I think that our answers to these questions don't matter; in fact, they matter deeply and should be considered faithfully. But what matters most of all is that (1) Jesus is proclaimed all in all; and (2) we recognize that wherever we take our stands, Jesus is kneeling among sinners on the other side of the lines we draw.

To us, and to them, he says, "Go and sin no more." All who meet him are forever changed.

* * *

John 4 tells another strange little story. This time, Jesus engages a Samaritan woman, an outsider to his own culture, at a well in Samaria. The story points to the abnormality of the interaction at a couple of different points. First, John makes sure that his readers know that the identity of the woman as a Samaritan, as well as her whole community, is something that would normally have erected a barrier; see the parenthetical "Jews do not share things in common with Samaritans" (John 4:9). Drawing on the recognized imagery of the "woman at the well" that appears throughout the Hebrew Bible (both Jacob and Moses met their wives at wells!), Jesus delivers his remarks about living water. The twist of the story is, that while he originally *asks* for living water, he himself *is* living water. Though the Samaritan woman serves him a cool drink of water, the water he can provide her, and all who would partake, is far more than what any person can supply.

It is only after this discussion of the living water, graciously offered to the Samaritan woman, that the discussion of the woman's past arises. Jesus instructs the woman to go and bring her husband back to the well: "The woman answered him, 'I have no husband.' Jesus said to her, 'You are right in saying, "I have no husband," for you have had five husbands, and the one you have now is not your husband. What you have said is true!'" (John 4:17–18).

This dialogue appears to question the woman's virtue and reputation. After all, she has had *five husbands*, with a possible sixth paramour, which seems to nullify any potential union she might have. Yet Jesus doesn't use this moment of exposure and vulnerability to condemn the woman, but rather to lead her to another realization about his own identity. Jesus' coming means that Jews and Samaritans no longer need to worship separately, Jews in the temple and Samaritans on the mountain, but that *all people* worship "in spirit and truth, for the Father seeks such as these to worship him" (John 4:23). This is followed by Jesus' revelation of his identity to the Samaritan woman that he is the Messiah.

The woman's experience of Jesus, particularly his divine knowledge of her complicated past, is the segue to her proclamation of the gospel: "Many Samaritans from that city believed in him because of the woman's testimony, 'He told me everything I have ever done'" (John 4:39). The woman's sexual past, however scandalous it might appear to others, doesn't preclude her from receiving the living water of Jesus, worshiping him, and ultimately, sharing the gospel message. In fact, it is *through* Jesus' engagement with her complicated story that the gospel is made known and shared.

It isn't that God overlooks our pasts and our wounds and says, "I don't care about those." Such words from God would probably feel flippant and even uncaring to us, as if God just doesn't want to take the time to listen to them. Rather, God knows, and knows so deeply that God chooses to share himself with us even more fully. Like the Samaritan woman's experience of Jesus at the well, God's intimate knowledge of us, without us even having to say a word, is what leads to

God's revelation to us. As fully as we might believe ourselves worthy of judgment—and speaking for myself, often I *am* reprehensible—what defines us isn't the parts of our stories that we'd change if we could. It's the divine encounter where Jesus shares himself and reclaims us as God's beloved children. It's not that the past doesn't matter, for Christ sees that, too, with eyes of love, eyes unashamed, and turns it all to love.

And what do we do, having met Jesus? We, like the Samaritan woman, go and tell our stories. We even tell the stories of how Jesus met us where we were, regardless and even because of how broken we were when we met him. Others will find the welcome that we too have found.

Five spouses deep, it isn't too late for Jesus to see us, know us, and welcome us into the feast, where we sit with all the other sinners, thieves, and beggars—that is, his followers.

* * *

One of Jesus' teachings in the Sermon on the Mount directly pertains to sexual immorality. Continuing the theme of "I haven't come to abolish the Law, but fulfill it" in Matthew 5, Jesus says:

> You have heard that it was said, "You shall not commit adultery." But I say to you that everyone who looks at a woman with lust has already committed adultery with her in his heart. If your right eye causes you to sin, tear it out and throw it away; it is better for you to lose one of your members than for your whole body to be thrown into hell. And if your right hand causes you to sin, cut it off and throw it away; it is better for you to lose one of

> your members than for your whole body to go into hell. (Matthew 5:27–30)

Frequently, women and girls in the church are instructed to dress modestly to avoid tempting men and boys who could be led astray by short skirts or spaghetti straps. But as much as Jesus' teachings are clear about anything, he's clear that lust is the responsibility of the lustful person to deal with. Lust is in the eye of the beholder, not created by the person who is its object.

Modesty can be valuable for its own sake, but it's not something to pursue because we're responsible for somebody else's purity. Most, if not all, of us experience sexual attraction. Even if we're married, attraction to someone other than a spouse is normal, or at least not uncommon. But the responsibility is in *how we respond* to our experiences of attraction.

What is most troublesome about lust, I think, is that it reduces a person to an object. Somebody we feel lust for is wanted as something we can possess. A person is not a possession but a vessel of divine worth. When lust leads us to reduce someone to an object, it is also so detrimental to our *own* bodies, minds, and souls that it's worth removing the organ that causes us to stumble.

It might seem like Jesus is setting the standard impossibly high. I've looked at more than a few men in my life and thought, "Dang, he's hot!" I don't think I'm alone in that, either. But lust takes attraction a step past noticing that someone is attractive. Lust is wanting a person physically for ourselves regardless of their circumstance in life, the needs and concerns of their mind and soul, and our own station in life and what's best for our mind and soul as well. Lust means that nothing matters besides the physical attraction that we feel for someone. They could really be anyone behind that attractive exterior. Lust says, "This person should be mine, and nothing else matters."

For those of us raised with the standards of purity culture, we can feel that we shouldn't be attracted to people. We shouldn't notice people at all. We should guard our bodies judiciously in modest bathing suits and long skirts lest we experience someone else's attraction for us (please note: I often wear modest bathing suits *and* long skirts, so far be it from me to knock that choice at all). We should bury our sexual attractions deep, deep, deep within us, deeper even than the gas we'd hate to pass in the presence of our admirers.

But attraction is God-given. We need attraction to tell us whom we're drawn to, whom we feel we might be able to get closer to and experience more of God through. It's human, and good, to appreciate the good things that God has made. One thing that I didn't realize as a young person, that I did learn as a married person, is that attraction doesn't magically turn off once we get married, either. We can be married and still notice people. But *acting* on attraction is always a choice. It's the job of each person who gazes to notice just on the perception level rather than moving it into the driver's seat of our psyches. We veer into the dangerous realm of lust when we see someone lovely or hunky and think, "It would be a *great* idea for me to take them to bed and do thus and so to them!" That isn't appreciating the good child of God that God has made, but rather seeking possession of another.

Honestly, lust is bad for the perceiver, too, which drives home Jesus' point about the harm to our own bodily integrity. Lust can mean we treat *ourselves* too poorly, like all we need for wholeness is a night in bed with somebody really attractive or somebody else's spouse. We need, and we deserve, so much more than that. Sexual intimacy is ideally for our own wholeness as well as the wholeness of another person. Yes, sex is supposed to be physically pleasurable, and something is probably askew if it's not, but indiscriminate sex doesn't generally make us happier. There's a lot of conflicting research about the connection between casual sex and depression, and it's hard to tell the chicken from the egg. Does risky sexual behavior like having multiple casual partners lead to depression, or does depression make risky sexual behaviors more likely? At least some studies find that in younger adults, increased amounts of casual sex can be linked with negative mental health symptoms.[2] It's ironic that what God designed for human fulfillment can often be reduced to so much less. What God designed to offer ultimate unity can result in disintegration of our mental health if driven by lust.

Theologically, Jesus' teachings about lust touch on what's so problematic with pornography. Pornography thrives on lust. Under the definition of lust that I've been operating with, pornography is the perfect case study of lust. Pornography removes, by design, all relational connection with the object of desire and replaces it with simple gratification. Pornography represents the antithesis of the self-giving and caregiving that God intends to be at the heart of a sexual relationship. I'm guessing that most viewers of pornography enjoy gazing at the person on the other side of the screen to serve their own sexual needs, while not thinking much about the humanity of that person as a beloved child of God. What gets the person performing sexual acts for the camera out of bed in the morning? What breaks their heart? What do they need to be well? Pornography gives sexual pleasure only through lust, which reduces another person to an object. (I further distinguish between pornography, which disconnects human beings from sexual acts, and child sexual abuse material, which is abhorrent and abusive.)

I'm a biblical theologian, not a psychologist, but from a theological perspective, it makes sense that receiving or seeking out purely physical resolution to the deepest longings of our souls is not adequate. Our physical attractions and desires point us to something so much more than what we can receive in casual sex. We are created for relationship—first of all with God, but also with human beings who can convey and represent to us the love of God made known incarnationally. We desire human partners to whom we can give ourselves fully, whom we can receive fully, and whom we can know and be known by as fully as humanly possible. *Of course* as mature sexual beings we yearn for connection in every way imaginable. *Of course* resolution of these desires by only physical means leaves us feeling empty. *Of course* God desires more for us that this.

So resist the lust that is for less than holistic union, Jesus tells us. Pluck out the eyes that threaten to give us less than what God desires for us, or what those people around us deserve. Jesus is seeking more for us, more, even, of the deep sexual desires that speak to our humanity, and not less. Never less.

3

Paul and the Early Church

PASSION AND CHASTITY

In a strong shift from Jesus, the apostle Paul talks quite a bit about sexuality, especially in 1 Corinthians 6–7. Because this is the most sustained discussion of sexuality in the Pauline epistles, it's worth a prolonged look. In it, Paul offers—even as an unmarried man—his understanding of the relationship of sexuality to the gospel of Jesus Christ, whom he exalts as the crucified and glorified one. If we're all to be conformed to Christ's crucifixion and resurrection, our sexuality, however we decide to live it out, must be included in this huge paradigm shift. The first lengthy passage in which Paul deals with sexuality in 1 Corinthians is this:

> "All things are permitted for me," but not all things are beneficial. "All things are permitted for me," but I will not be dominated by anything. "Food is meant for the stomach and the stomach for food," and God will destroy both one and the other. The body is meant not for sexual immorality but for the Lord and the Lord for the body. And God raised the Lord and will also raise us by his power. Do you not know

> that your bodies are members of Christ? Should I therefore take the members of Christ and make them members of a prostitute? Never! Do you not know that whoever is united to a prostitute becomes one body with her? For it is said, "The two shall be one flesh." But anyone united to the Lord becomes one spirit with him. Shun sexual immorality! Every sin that a person commits is outside the body, but the sexually immoral person sins against the body itself. Or do you not know that your body is a temple of the Holy Spirit within you, which you have from God, and that you are not your own? For you were bought with a price; therefore glorify God in your body. (1 Corinthians 6:12–20)

The ethic of sexuality in this passage rests on the metaphor "Your body is a temple of the Holy Spirit within you." To understand what Paul means by this, we need to consider why Paul uses the temple as his reference point. As beautiful as this image intrinsically sounds, there are multiple levels to consider.

First, the temple is good. The temple is created as a site to gather and worship God, to house the dwelling place of God. The temple is worthy of the utmost care and protection.

The temple is built with care, intention, and specifications. Everything in the temple is beautiful and created for a sacred purpose, mirroring what is in heaven. We are not made the way we are carelessly or by accident, but designed by a Creator who loves us.

There are different levels of access that different people enjoy to different parts of the temple. There are times and seasons of access, and times and seasons of restriction. Only a select few pass into the holy of holies; those who violate these boundaries face dire consequences. Only the priest enters the holy of holies, and only on Yom Kippur, the Jewish Day of Atonement.

But there's also a precarity to this metaphor. The temple can be ransacked and harmed. The cataclysmic cultural events of the Hebrew Bible center on the destruction of the temple as a cultural icon and sacred center. The temple is sacred, but it is also vulnerable. It can break. It can be despoiled.

We know this because 1 Corinthians 6 isn't the only place in the Bible that compares the body and the temple. In Lamentations, the city of Jerusalem, also known as Zion, is portrayed as a woman, who talks about her own experiences:

> Her uncleanness was in her skirts;
> she took no thought of her future;
> her downfall was appalling,
> with none to comfort her.
> Look, O Lord, at my affliction,
> for the enemy has triumphed!
>
> Enemies have stretched out their hands
> over all her precious things;
> she has even seen the nations
> invade her sanctuary,
> those whom you forbade
> to enter your congregation. (Lamentations 1:9–10)

One of the experiences that Zion recounts is being bodily assailed by human invaders. The connection with sexual assault is inescapable. The woman's body is the temple, and the temple is desecrated even in the most sacred spaces. First the Babylonian invasion, and later, Roman enforcement of imperial authority, will mean that the temple is destroyed—twice. The body and the temple are intricately linked in the poetic imagination of the writing. Desecrating the temple is like violating a body. Violating a body is like desecrating a temple.

But in 1 Corinthians, we can imagine what it would be like for the body to be venerated like a sacred site, too; a temple that stands and is not sacrilegiously demolished. What if the interactions between two people, or even one person individually, could truly treat the body like a place where the Holy Spirit can dwell?

Sexual immorality, no matter how we understand it, is wrong because it hurts our own body, our own temple. It's wrong because it hurts another person's temple. But what is right glorifies God. For those of us who have been raised in purity culture, can we even imagine a way of understanding our sexuality, our divine createdness, as glorifying God?

All of this is also tied to Paul's idea that all who are within the church are members of the body of Christ. The body of Christ is the fullest manifestation of the "temple of the Holy Spirit" imaginable, because the Holy Spirit is fully present in the person of Jesus Christ, the Son of God. Yet we, too, are members of the body, each of us reflections of the One who gives life to the world.

The reflections of spiritual mystics invite us to understand the intimate connection between our bodies and that of Christ. One of my favorite blessings was written by the mystic Saint Teresa of Avila:

> Christ has no body but yours,
> No hands, no feet on earth but yours,
> Yours are the eyes with which he looks
> Compassion on this world,
> Yours are the feet with which he walks to do good,
> Yours are the hands, with which he blesses all the world.
> Yours are the hands, yours are the feet,
> Yours are the eyes, you are his body.

> Christ has no body now but yours,
> No hands, no feet on earth but yours,
> Yours are the eyes with which he looks
> compassion on this world.
> Christ has no body now on earth but yours.[1]

Knowing that we are bearing Christ's body, how do we then live our lives as sexual beings in this world? How does knowing that we are members of Christ's body compel us to relate to ourselves and one another? For starters, respect of ourselves and others comes to mind. We need to venerate the human body as first and foremost the temple of God and Christ's body, and we have no inherent right to anyone else's. We can have confidence and pride in the ways that our bodies, no matter how fragile, wonky, or disabled, carry Christ into the world.

MARRYING SO WE DON'T BURN

One of my college professors told a great story about a wedding she officiated where the couple planned for the famous 1 Corinthians 13 chapter to be read aloud ("Love is patient, love is kind . . .") but the reader made a mistake and started in boldly on some of Paul's more strident words against marriage: "But if they are not practicing self-control, they should marry. For it is better to marry than to be aflame with passion" (1 Corinthians 7:9). Congratulations to the happy couple—and enjoy marriage as an alternative to burning with lust! Paul clearly doesn't consider marriage to be the ideal state, as he, like Jesus, was a single man.

In context, the fuller passage from 1 Corinthians 7 reads:

> Concerning the matters about which you wrote: "It is good for a man not to touch a woman." But because of cases of sexual immorality, each man should have his own wife and

> each woman her own husband. The husband should give to his wife what is due her and likewise the wife to her husband. For the wife does not have authority over her own body, but the husband does; likewise, the husband does not have authority over his own body, but the wife does. Do not deprive one another except perhaps by agreement for a set time, to devote yourselves to prayer, and then come together again, so that Satan may not tempt you because of your lack of self-control. This I say by way of concession, not of command. I wish that all were as I myself am. But each has a particular gift from God, one having one kind and another a different kind.
>
> To the unmarried and the widows I say that it is good for them to remain unmarried as I am. But if they are not practicing self-control, they should marry. For it is better to marry than to be aflame with passion. (1 Corinthians 7:1–9)

Though our twenty-first-century notions of sexuality likely feel some tension with this passage, note that its overwhelming emphasis is toward enthusiastic self-giving. Sexuality is not pleasurable or consensual if it's begrudging. For those who are not made of the same metal as Paul, and cannot simply be abstinent, the vision of sexuality in marriage is that it's freely given and fair. We are to willingly give ourselves to our marriage partner not because one partner is subordinate to the other, but because we *both* belong to each other. Notice how "the wife does not have authority over her own body" and "the husband does not have authority over his own body." Marriage is designed to be a situation of mutual self-giving of both partners.

This relationship of equality is presupposed for the mutual self-giving of marriage. Paul is *not* talking about a violent relationship in which one or both partners is abusing the other.

A relationship where one partner doesn't see themselves as "belonging to" the other but is instead harming and exploiting the other is not really a marriage, and it can't continue for that reason.

Nor does Paul seem to think that one or both marriage partners are bad people if, for a time, they don't have sex. In married relationships, there are inevitably times when two people cannot come together, whether due to travel, restrictions in high-risk pregnancies, healing after birth or other medical events, emotional trauma, or simply the development of the relationship over time. As precious a gift as sex is, marital intimacy is more than just sex. But the key here is communication. Both people in the marriage should have the security of knowing that their partner is not self-withholding for reasons of wanting to harm the other.

Paul's conflicted perspective on marriage stems from how he thought about the timeline for the world's end. He believed Jesus was coming back soon, so bonds like marriage were temporary at best. The better focus for believers, he thought, was to exercise discipline toward preparing oneself for the imminent return of Christ.

And maybe it's because of Paul's complicated views about marriage that he interweaves a metaphor of marriage into his discourses on the relationship between the law and the Christian. He writes of the temporality of marriage as the way toward understanding how the law is to shape us as believers:

> Do you not know, brothers and sisters—for I am speaking to those who know the law—that the law is binding on a person only during that person's lifetime? Thus a married woman is bound by the law to her husband as long as he lives, but if her husband dies, she is discharged from the law

> concerning the husband. Accordingly, she will be called an adulteress if she belongs to another man while her husband is alive. But if her husband dies, she is free from that law, and if she belongs to another man, she is not an adulteress.
>
> In the same way, my brothers and sisters, you have died to the law through the body of Christ, so that you may belong to another, to him who was raised from the dead in order that we may bear fruit for God. For while we were living in the flesh, our sinful passions, aroused by the law, were at work in our members to bear fruit for death. But now we are discharged from the law, dead to that which held us captive, so that we are enslaved in the newness of the Spirit and not in the oldness of the written code. (Romans 7:1–6)

There's a lot going on here regarding Paul's theology of the law, and how it's good but not permanent, binding but not eternal, but more than that, I'd like to focus on Paul's description of married love. Paul talks about marriage as a kind of bondage; it isn't the ultimate good for Paul. He also refers to sex as a kind of belonging: "Accordingly, she will be called an adulteress if she belongs to another man while her husband is alive" (Romans 7:3). Notice, this adultery isn't about a wife belonging to another husband in marriage; this would not be legally possible while one is still married. Rather, because adultery has to do with sex, it is *sex* that Paul thinks can also give us belonging to one another.

So what can we take from Paul's writings about sex? First, sex is serious business for Paul, and for him, it belongs within the context of marriage as a seal for the covenant between two people. Marriage is binding, and sex is part of a unique relationship between married partners. Sex, for Paul, involves total self-giving. A husband belongs to a wife; a wife belongs to a husband. The physical union of sex represents a much more profound spiritual covenant.

But sex (and, of course, marriage) isn't for everybody, and it doesn't represent the pinnacle of human existence. Paul understands union with God as the most important connection that we can experience, and he personally decides to devote himself to the divine relationship instead of pursuing a more traditional route of having a family. Paul therefore frees us from limiting our understanding of intimacy to human terms. For people who are single, either by choice or by circumstance, this may be a freeing reality. Neither for Jesus nor for Paul does union with a sexual partner define the worth of one's life. In fact, people who live outside the more conventional sexual relationships may have more freedom to pursue the proclamation of the gospel. But most of us are, to use Paul's terminology, "burning," and marital commitment empowers us to channel our desire into building a lifelong love with another person. This love *should* help us steer clear of treating someone else as an object.

THE CHURCH TAKES SHAPE

Since Jesus didn't come back as quickly as anticipated, a lot more structure around things like family life became necessary to order life for his followers. What would marriage in the cruciform life look like? How would society arrange itself to reflect godly values and hierarchies? Much like the books of the Law in the Old Testament that sought to establish and maintain Israelite distinctiveness while the Israelites were surrounded by more powerful empires and peoples, the early church also had to maintain distinctiveness from the Roman Empire around it. Still, the early church was also influenced by and drew profoundly from its Greco-Roman context.

As the church took shape, sexual roles became more defined and prescriptive. One of the classic texts for talking about married love is Ephesians 5, in which the ordering of society seems to follow precedents from Roman society. Male landowners trump the power and authority of everyone else, and women come before enslaved people, but not by terribly much. However, at least in married love, the emphasis is on mutual submission. In the patriarchal society of the time, men were authoritative over women. So the idea of mutual submission could have felt challenging to the Ephesians. That's a difference from today's audience, for whom the word *submission* can be understandably jarring.

No doubt, the writer of Ephesians has a different idea of the relationship between a husband and wife than many people of our time, with the husband as the "head" of the wife (Ephesians 5:23), but the writer still envisions a powerful interconnection that goes beyond the physical into the emotional, intellectual, and spiritual. We can hope for a connection with another person that leads us into giving ourselves over completely to the other.

As much as the "submission" part of the passage may catch our attention, Paul actually dwells longer on what it means for a loving, godly husband to exist within the relationship: "Husbands should love their wives as their own bodies. He who loves his wife loves himself. For no one ever hates his own flesh, but he nourishes and tenderly cares for it, just as Christ does for the church, because we are members of his body" (Ephesians 5:28–30).

Practically, what would husbands "loving their wives as they love themselves" look like for believers? It means, at the very least, that the desire for satisfaction or pleasure can never be one-sided. We'll talk a lot more about pleasure in a later chapter, but the concept of mutual love means very profoundly that nothing, physically or otherwise, should be done for the main or exclusive benefit of oneself. In a society where men could easily out-rule women both socially and politically, this is truly revolutionary. Where men could ignore women's needs and wants inside and outside the marriage bed, instead they're to be every bit as self-sacrificial as women. The uplift and wellness of the other is always to be the point.

The upshot of all of this *mutual* love and *mutual* self-giving is that it images for the world the love of Christ for the church. The marital bond between two people is so immense that it provides a model for the mysterious dance of love between the trinity of Father, Son, and Holy Spirit. It is truly amazing that our physical selves can illustrate that love.

AFTER THE END

Those who endure the many sufferings of the end times in Revelation will enjoy their status as the bride of Christ, united to him through a marriage that is celebrated at a great banquet:

> Let us rejoice and exult
>   and give him the glory,
> for the marriage of the Lamb has come,
>   and his bride has made herself ready;
> to her it has been granted to be clothed
>   with fine linen, bright and pure. (Revelation 19:7–8)

Much like Isaiah writing about the realization of God's reign, the apocalyptic writer of Revelation describes how the faithful will unite with God in a beautiful reunion that can be best expressed as a marriage. All people who are in Christ are his bride. Just as Israel was understood to be the bride of YHWH, adorned, adored, and chosen, so now the church is understood to fulfill the role of the woman in the marriage feast of the Lamb.

Our human sexual relationships can only dimly mirror the glory of the relationship that the apocalyptic writer imagines. But the resemblance in faulty, fallen human relationships is significant enough that the writer of Revelation chooses them to model the love of Christ. We know that we fail to get the consummation of human erotic love right much of the time. I know that my own journey reveals the depth of how hard we can fail. But we strive to because, I think, most of us believe that such a beautiful, divine union is still possible.

So how do we try? In the remaining chapters, I want to delve into some of the questions we face as we prepare to teach the next generation about sexuality. Rooting sexuality in the love of Jesus means far more than zeroing in on his few teachings directly related to sexuality, which we've already covered.

The resounding message for me from the New Testament boils down to this: Love God, and love others. When Jesus is asked what the greatest commandment is, this is what he has to say:

> "You shall love the Lord your God with all your heart and with all your soul and with all your mind." This is the greatest and first commandment. And a second is like it: "You shall love your neighbor as yourself." On these two commandments hang all the Law and the Prophets. (Matthew 22:37–40)

Loving God and loving our neighbors and loving ourselves (and Jesus is very explicit that we are among those to be included in our own love) is what matters to God. And if this teaching is really at the core of the Law and the Prophets, then maybe there's a way to wade through everything else.

PART II

Loving God, Others, And Ourselves

4

Doing Just Us Justice

CONFIDENCE IN PERSONAL IDENTITY

The great commandment gives us a huge task: to figure out how to love everybody, including God, well. It's intimidating, actually, when I come down to it. And it can be even more intimidating when we try to apply that teaching to our sex lives, which, we can hope, are not an unimportant part of life. How, then, can the sexual lives that we have, and that we teach to our kids, center this great love of self and other?

After all, both physicality and emotion are interwoven in that great commandment that Jesus centers, to love God with all our mind, and soul, and strength, and to love our neighbors as well. But, Jesus reminds us, we can love our neighbors only to the extent that we have learned to love ourselves. That is not easy for many of us. We struggle to even like ourselves, let alone love ourselves. We try to avoid coming face-to-face with ourselves so many times over. Our weight, our hair, the decisions we've made in the past, the scars that we carry—all of these and more affect how we see ourselves.

Sometimes it seems so much easier to love ourselves when we are small children. I've seen this firsthand as a parent. My first child in particular came into her life with confidence oozing from her pores. When she was two, she'd walk into a room and shout, "HELLO, WORLD! DEBBIE JOY IS HERE NOW!" She owned the heck out of her presence on this earth. I hope and pray she always keeps that confidence, but I can already see some shadows of adolescence in her friend group that make me think that maybe self-possession is not always so easy.

One of the greatest challenges and gifts as a parent, particularly for me as a single parent, is recognizing that the ways I see myself and treat myself are likely the ways that my daughters will see themselves and talk about themselves. By extension, the ways that I relate to partners will likely become the ways that they will relate to partners. For me, this has meant that I have ended two marriages. That, maybe surprisingly, was the relatively easy part. The harder part is the maintenance of a lifestyle and outlook that I want to pass along when the day-to-day struggle of life is so much. But when I can take the time to exercise, to make a meal that fuels my body well, to spend time in prayer, to put on a special outfit that I feel good in, *my girls notice*. And the best part is when my four-year-old daughter notices and asks, "Mommy, why are you doing that?" And I say, "Because I want to feel good!"

Those moments are only sometimes, and fewer and further between than I wish they were, but I still think they're powerful. I hope that my girls will learn from me that though I do struggle on a regular basis, I love myself. That the love they see in those moments is not a facade; today, as I am squarely in my mid-thirties, it is easier to love and accept myself than it has ever been before. It is easier to advocate for myself than it has ever been. It is easier to thank God for creating me in the weird, idiosyncratic ways that I am, and even for the twists and turns in my story that have led here.

It isn't that I get it right all the time; I don't. But I have realized that without God creating me the way I am, I would not have had the ability or honor to accompany certain neighbors in my work. I have beheld my daughters and realized that without me as their mom, they would be different people, too.

I think that the self-love that we're searching for is closer than we think it is, and we don't need a new skin care regime, juice cleanse, or six-pack to embrace ourselves. This self-love begins with a deep understanding of who we are in relation to God, a deep understanding of who we were always created to be. From the first moments of existence, before we were even a sparkle in our mothers' eyes, God knew us and loved us. In the first of the two creation stories in the opening chapters of Genesis, God creates humanity *after* everyone, saving what can be most closely in relationship with God for the very last. God creates humanity, both male and female, in the "image" and "likeness" of God. The whole sequence is repeated in Genesis 1:26–27, just in case we missed it the first time:

> Then God said, "Let us make humans in our image, according to our likeness, and let them have dominion over the fish of the sea and over the birds of the air and over the cattle and over all the wild animals of the earth and over every creeping thing that creeps upon the earth."
>
> So God created humans in his image,
> in the image of God he created them;
> male and female he created them. (Genesis 1:26–27)

We are created for intimacy. We are also created for authority. Every single one of us.

The words *image* and *likeness* would have rung bells for many ancient readers in the ways that they echoed ancient Near Eastern concepts of kingship. In some ancient Near Eastern mythologies, the kings were understood to be made "in the image" of the gods. So the Genesis story takes this idea and runs with it, but extends the concept *to all people.* Not just the kings were made in the image of the divine, but every single person who walks on this earth.

What does this mean, practically? We are all bearers of the divine. Our hearts, minds, souls, and strengths were all made to carry the image of God into the world. If someone wants to know what God is like, they are supposed to be able to look, in some form or fashion, at us.

And we are not just made, abstractly and impersonally, in God's image. We are animated intimately and personally by the Holy Spirit. The second creation story tells the story of the creation of humans in a slightly different way. This time, God touches us. God is the potter; we are the clay: "Then the LORD God formed man from the dust of the ground and breathed into his nostrils the breath of life, and the man became a living being. And the LORD God planted a garden in Eden, in the east, and there he put the man whom he had formed" (Genesis 2:7–8). I hope that this image, of God breathing into the nostrils of the man and giving us life, never leaves any one of us. God cares so personally about us that God gives the first human some kind of divine CPR to bring us to life.

In the second creation story, the woman is created separately, but second. (Again, the principle of "saving the best for last" might apply.) God continues his medical prowess, putting the man to sleep and extracting the raw materials from the man's ribs to form the woman. From the very beginning, humans are created for intimate relationships with God and each other. We do not exist without each other. We are one another's "fitting helpers," made not for subservience to one another but for loving communion. People are created to need each other to thrive. For God says, "It is not good for the man to be alone." Something about the man is created for community with the other.

We need each other. We're not created to be alone. But at the same time, we need to have a sense of who we are outside of the other. We need to know how much we are precious, loved, and valued without the external validation of the other. Will we ever get there, fully? Probably not, and we don't need to pretend that external validation is irrelevant to us. Yet we need to know that validation by a romantic or sexual partner is not what gives our lives meaning and purpose. I've experienced the pain of relationships where one person believed the other was necessary to keep the other alive. Those were the most volatile and dangerous relationships that I've ever been a part of. To a less dramatic extreme, it can be easy for many people, myself included, to jump from relationship to relationship out of a sense of loneliness. It's easy also to exchange sex for a sense of belonging and security.

Even though that feeling of need makes sense, we need to anchor our souls in something more firm and secure than the fallibilities of another person. Other people can change, withdraw affection, or set boundaries in ways that limit our access. These may all be healthy and necessary actions. In a truly secure relationship, we'll be able to know who we are even while intimate with somebody else.

Beyond the creation stories, the Scriptures display God's intimate love for us from the beginning. God knows us and loves us exactly how we are. Sometimes, we may feel like Jeremiah, standing before a calling but believing that we can never be good enough. Within this relatable experience, God assures Jeremiah that he absolutely belongs in his calling. God says:

> "Before I formed you in the womb I knew you,
> and before you were born I consecrated you;
> I appointed you a prophet to the nations."
> Then [Jeremiah] said, "Ah, Lord God! Truly I do not know how to speak, for I am only a boy." But the LORD said to me,
> "Do not say, 'I am only a boy,'
> for you shall go to all to whom I send you,
> and you shall speak whatever I command you.
> Do not be afraid of them,
> for I am with you to deliver you,
> says the LORD." (Jeremiah 1:5–8)

One mark of prophetic call stories is how the prophet says "Nope, not me, Lord, miss me with that" before God unveils the ways that he will be with the prophet and the prophet finds it within him or her to say yes. Jonah, Moses, Isaiah, Jeremiah—"not me" seems to be the most natural response to a call from God. If we feel inadequate today to respond to God's call, we are most certainly not alone. But God does not ask of us something outside of who we are. God calls us to manifest the glory of God that is already within us, to live out God's power and love in a broken or hurting world. In these verses from Jeremiah, God never denies any of what Jeremiah says about himself. He *is* a boy when he is called. But God also makes a point that God calls him *in his infancy*: "Before I formed you in the womb I knew you, and before you were born I consecrated you; I appointed you a prophet to the nations." Jeremiah's only problem, in God's eyes, is speaking poorly of himself in his youth. In the very situation, in the very personhood where he is, God calls Jeremiah to be a messenger of justice and love.

God calls each of us as we are, too, including in the sexual domains of our lives. In the words of Ephesians, "I, therefore, the prisoner in the Lord, beg you to walk in a manner worthy of the calling to which you have been called, with all humility and gentleness, with patience, bearing with one another in love, making every effort to maintain the unity of the Spirit in the bond of peace" (Ephesians 4:1-3). As people striving to carry ourselves as healthy and whole people, we can hold our heads high. We *are* worthy of the calling to which we've be called, even when we don't feel like it, because God has called us there. We are valuable as human beings, first of all, created in God's image, but we are also valuable in the particularities in which the image of God becomes manifest in our lives. To "walk worthy of this calling," we can hold our heads high in the world while we also love and serve, knowing that God has given us ourselves to be part of the kingdom in some way so mysterious and important that only God may know.

I have sometimes heard the question asked, "How can you expect anyone to love you if you don't love yourself first?" There's probably a nugget of truth to this, but that's not really what I'm suggesting, and at its core, I don't think this phrase reflects the deepest truth about ourselves either. The point is not that we have to be good enough, worthy enough of other people's love—including making ourselves worthy by loving ourselves. Regardless of how we feel about ourselves, how good or bad we think we are, God loves us first. God chooses us first. Two thousand years ago, Jesus died for the love of each of us—and even if there were *just one of us* on this whole earth, he would have died for love of that one person. We don't need to look at ourselves first to generate love of ourselves. We need only look at God revealed in Christ, whose love is so apparent through the stories passed down through sacred tradition and who meets us still today through our communities, sacraments, and prayers.

I'm definitely not the poster child for radical self-acceptance. Though it's easier to accept myself than it was when I was a teenager, it is a vulnerable thing to be a human alive on this earth. The words that others say to us can linger longer than the speaker ever intended them to. When I was thirteen or fourteen at a church retreat, another girl said to me, "You would be pretty . . . if you wore makeup." I tried to play it cool, like I didn't care whether I was pretty or not, like I took the compliment without hearing the imbedded insult (intended or not). "Oh, thanks," I tried to say breezily, "I don't really want to wear makeup." Shortly after, I went back to my cabin and cried in humiliation because I was pretty sure no boy would ever want to kiss a girl who would be pretty—if she wore makeup.

A current social media trend is to write a post about meeting your younger self for coffee, mentioning details like what the current and younger version of yourself would order, who would arrive first, how the past and present would lovingly embrace, what sentimental tears would be shed, and so on. To indulge the trend for just a moment (we all know I'd be early because my always-on-time mother would drop me off), I would probably have to balance my empathy for my easily embarrassed younger self with a swift reality check. If she were in a brutally honest mood, she'd confide in me about how sometimes she worries late at night that she will never be kissed, that a boy will never want her, and that the people who said she'd always be alone were actually right. "I know I'm smart," my younger self would say. "But I'm not sure I'm actually pretty." "Dude," I'd whisper to the girl across the table, "getting boys to kiss you is never going to be the problem. The problem is kissing them because you really want to and like them, not just because it's the thing the moment socially calls for or the thing that'll earn you a secure-feeling place in warm arms. Please, for the love of all things holy, realize how powerful and smart and beautiful you are before you go looking for love where you don't want to find it."

There were those who definitely tried to let me know. A youth minister introduced me to Psalm 139 when I was seventeen (I know, I didn't grow up in the most Bible-literate congregation). As I meditated on the words of the psalm, I came to realize, for the first time maybe, what it would mean to live like I was really and truly loved by God.

> For it was you who formed my inward parts;
>   you knit me together in my mother's womb.
> I praise you, for I am fearfully and wonderfully made.
>   Wonderful are your works;
> that I know very well.
>   My frame was not hidden from you,
> when I was being made in secret,
>   intricately woven in the depths of the earth.
> Your eyes beheld my unformed substance.
> In your book were written
>   all the days that were formed for me,
>   when none of them as yet existed. (Psalm 139:13–16)

As a physically insecure teenager, this psalm affected me as I began to understand, little by little, that I was made and designed by a God who really knew me. I was not made by accident. The physical features that made me insecure were known and accepted by God, and even lovingly designed. I was lovingly shaped by a potter God who imagined me and knew me perfectly well even before my own mother did. The things about myself that I struggled to love belonged also to God, to whom they were not unlovable, but loved from the very beginning.

If I want to say that the *other* works of God are wonderful—whether the crashing ocean waves that deafen me, my nieces and nephews and my own babies, or the songs of joy that ring out on Easter morning to herald the news of the risen Lord—if *these* are the thoughts of God that are "so wonderful" to me, then are the thoughts of God that resulted in me not to be commended too? Doesn't it diminish our praise of God's amazing thoughts, by which he speaks the world into being, if we harshly critique the thoughts that make ourselves as well?

And that is why, I believe, the writer narrows the focus from speaking just about the "works" in the abstract to the full manifestation of works in the psalmist's very being. From the psalmist's gestation inside a mother's womb, God has known the psalmist through and through. There's nothing to be ashamed of before God, nothing to hide. It feels too good to be true, but it's the truest thing in the world that the perfect, infinite, powerful God of all knows us fully, and loves us, not anyway, but because of who we are. And so the psalmist exclaims, in full disbelief:

> How weighty to me are your thoughts, O God!
> How vast is the sum of them!
> I try to count them—they are more than the sand;
> I come to the end—I am still with you. (Psalm 139:17–18)

It is indeed weighty to feel the full sum of God's goodness, not indirectly to some foreign land or distant glow of sunrise, but within our fragile, finite frames. It is weighty to know that God desired us enough to make us, not as some perfect and naturally chaste and abstract being, but as the fleshly creatures we are. God could have made us all supermodels. God could have made us without any desire for intimacy, even. Yet most people do desire to be known and loved in the arms of a partner.

Because even our sexual design reflects God's creation of all of us in God's image. God chose sexual relationship as a way that God would be revealed in us, showing God's majesty to the world.

To really do God's creation justice, it needs to be just us. We need to know that God created us as pinnacles of light and love just as we are, all the flaws and imperfections we fret about included. We need to know that we have a place in God's heart even without a human companion to share the intimacy of divine love.

For many of us, one of the most difficult things we can do is to look in the mirror and see ourselves, however we are, as a beloved child of God. We live in a culture where digital filters, Botox, and fad diets teach us that our lovability is limited by how closely we conform to an arbitrary standard of beauty. Whiteness, typical ability, thinness, and youth are all attributes prized by the North American culture where I live, and it's easy to think that this standard is *the* way things should be. But most people don't fit this mythical model. Even people who come closer than many others to fitting this model often don't think that they do. I can remember many times being completely flabbergasted by learning that thin white women with perfect hair and makeup felt like their bodies were inadequate, that they suffered from anxiety or depression or eating disorders because they simply felt like they weren't good enough. If those women I was looking at in envy, who seemed outwardly to have it all together, were somehow struggling with even more insecurity than I was, then who in the world *was* truly secure in their selfhood?

Indeed, the symptoms of our cultural self-hatred are endemic, but the irony is that we can feel so alone in thinking that we are not enough, in seeking ways to change ourselves away from what is good, holy, and natural. For example, women can internalize a pressure to "bounce back" after childbirth, to be physically the exact same way we were before. Speaking from personal experience, birthing a nine-pound baby and a couple other seven-pounders after that has changed me more than I'm sometimes comfortable with. Absolutely, experiences like childbirth affect us as physical, emotional, intellectual, spiritual, and yes, sexual beings—and we can bravely allow them to.

There's beauty not just in the mores of culture that we've internalized, but in the bodies where our journeys with God have brought us. The softness and squishiness of my belly that was not there before I had children probably wouldn't earn me a place in *Playboy* magazine, but they reflect how I've helped to birth the kingdom of God in my life. The sagging of my breasts probably wouldn't lend itself well to a plunging neckline, but this is the body that has nourished three small children. The scars on my arm from the surgery I had when I was twelve may mean my skin isn't flawless, but they remind me how God has been with me through my deepest fears. The white patches on my arms from my autoimmune condition mean that wearing a tank top can make me feel insecure, but they remind me that my friends' love for me isn't contingent on blending in with the crowd.

We accept treatment that is less than what we deserve because we buy into the narratives that we are not enough. Please hear me, though, that it *is not our fault if we do experience bad treatment; our insecurity does not justify abuse, ever*. If someone takes advantage of our honest vulnerability, we can sometimes find ourselves bound to them longer than we want to be because we may feel that nobody else will ever want us, that we don't deserve any better, or that we are in some way obligated to continue supplying the needs of those who exploit us. We commercialize sexuality and tie it to people who match what we see on social media. We fear that we cannot be desired or accepted as we are.

So many of us, whether young or old, give in to the lowest bidder for our bodies and hearts. What if we knew that the highest bidder was God, always, first, and last? What if the next highest bidder was always ourselves, believing in our sacred worth, grounded in a new identity? What then would we do?

I suspect the answer would be different for all of us. But I suspect that for most of us, sexual choices based on fear of rejection would be gone. I suspect that many of us would wait longer for our first sexual encounters than we actually did. I suspect that we wouldn't be bound in unhealthy relationships because we don't feel like we deserve any better.

It's easy to conclude that a gospel based on self-love is just a fluffy, self-serving, personally therapeutic way of neutralizing the way of Jesus. But that's not what I'm saying. The point is not whether we'd like ourselves if we encountered ourselves on, say, my favorite train from South Bend to Chicago. The point is that God loved us first. The point is that as much as it might seem self-abnegating to be hypercritical of ourselves, the way we treat ourselves will bleed into the way we treat other people too. Turns out it's actually super hard to love our neighbors when we are incapable of loving ourselves.

I see it as a mom all the time. My daughters replicate the language I use about myself, others, and the world. The attitudes I hold and the aphorisms I repeat are the same ones my daughters start using. Currently, I find myself saying, "We build up, we don't tear down" all the time as sibling squabbles threaten to get out of hand. My youngest daughter, currently age four, loves to tattle on her sisters with a heartfelt, high-pitched, "MOMMY, GABBY'S TEARING ME DOWN!" And all this means that I must be very careful, even in my frustrations about my own limitations and insecurities, to try not to give those attitudes to my daughters. We recently had a friend over for dinner who referred to himself as possibly "fat" if he ate more at dinner, and I reactively hissed at him, "We don't say that word about ourselves!" He looked at me like I was out of my mind, which, honestly, I probably am. But the point stands, I think: how can we expect others to love and live into their Christian vocations when we cannot love ourselves?

Our closest relationships set the tone for all other relationships in our lives. Our parents, yes, our siblings, sure—but our relationships with ourselves matter deeply too. If we have a fractured sense of identity, if we rely on other people rather than God's love to tell us who we are, if we feel contempt and disgust for ourselves—how can that *not* shape the way we sexually relate to others, even and especially when we attempt to form lifelong partnerships? If we really want to love our neighbors, the first step might be to learn how to love ourselves in a healthy, holistic way. Loving ourselves does not mean ignoring the fact we have flaws. Loving ourselves does not mean thinking we're better than anyone else; Lord knows that's not true, either. But learning to love ourselves means seeing ourselves, no matter what, as clothed in the love with which God surrounds us from before we were born.

Our sexual identities are one aspect of being created in the image of God. Our thirst for connection mirrors the character of God, who created humans out of a desire for communion with creation. Even the parts of our sexuality that may make us insecure—as some people may feel about the size or appearance of their external sexual organs, for example—are a grace of God. Our desires to be known and touched and held are not shameful. Our desire for pleasure, even, is not shameful. None of these things related to our sexual identities are bad, and it is God's grace that we yearn for relationship with others in these ways.

I don't think we have to be wholly healed before we're in relationship with another person, sexually or otherwise. If we were wholly healed of all our earthly maladies, we'd be in heaven, right? But I do think that beginning the process of healing our relationship with our spirits, our bodies, ourselves, needs to begin before we start looking for fulfillment through romantic partners telling us that we matter.

If we cannot reconcile ourselves to the image of God within us, we risk being busheled. As Jesus says in the Sermon on the Mount, our light, the light of Christ, is to shine for the whole world to see:

> You are the light of the world. A city built on a hill cannot be hid. People do not light a lamp and put it under the bushel basket; rather, they put it on the lampstand, and it gives light to all in the house. In the same way, let your light shine before others, so that they may see your good works and give glory to your Father in heaven. (Matthew 5:14–16)

We need to know that we, ourselves, carry the light. We don't need a relationship to shine for us. We don't need to wait to shine until we have a relationship. We shine because Jesus says we do, speaking long ago to his audience on a Palestinian hill and now to us today. If the light of Christ is in us, it cannot stop shining from us. Let nothing cover this light. Don't try to hide in smallness or fear. Live your life big—whether that means, for you, loving your life reading novels and watching romcoms in your free moments (wait, that's probably me, not you) or going salsa dancing on Wednesday nights at the community center. Let that light be bright for all to see. Celebrate that light within you—and love yourself, the way that God made you. Because a relationship, sexual or otherwise, of two people who have learned to love themselves is powerful. Two people who are secure in the love of God for them and within them will create health in their relationship.

So my encouragement is to seek first the kingdom of God as single and healing people. Seek first the knowledge about who we are, what we need, and what we have to offer the world. I believe that everything else we can ever need and want follows from this deep rootedness.

For some of us, this desire to know ourselves first may lead us to seasons of abstinence. But let's not regard abstinence as a mark of fear or shame. Let us choose to abstain until we feel that we understand and appreciate the light within us, that we have shone with and for Christ without a partner, not because we think that sex is dirty or because we are ashamed to share ourselves with someone else.

And when we choose to become sexually intimate, let it not be because we feel we're not enough on our own. Let it not be because we are too lonely without a partner. Let it be because we know and respect our own light, radiating our brightness through the darkness of our world so much that we cannot help but share that light with someone else.

5

The Space Between Us

LOVE AND BOUNDARIES

As a kid and as a younger woman, I don't think I ever really learned how to say no. I was a classically polite, quiet, homeschooled kid—except sometimes with my family, as I'm sure they'd waste no time in telling you. But typically, I was obedient. I was respectful. Grownups liked me. My peers thought I was sweet. Especially as a young person with a significant trauma history, saying no could also feel scary to me. Through my twenties, I became increasingly afraid that saying no—to anything—could have negative consequences. "No" could even feel like a word that didn't exist for me in the sexual realm.

Enter Susannah 2.0, mom edition. I've often said that being a mother has helped me find strength and courage for myself. Knowing that my three girls rely on me for protection and wellness has meant that even when I might have been afraid to say no for me, I have had the courage to say no for them. Including when it's been very costly.

So imagine my shock and horror when one of my children came home from her daycare at age three saying that the teacher taught her, "We don't say no to grownups." I get it, on one level. Three kids are a lot for me to handle on my own as a single mom, and I would be completely lost in a classroom of seventeen or more pint-sized minions. Obedience matters a lot in every context, but especially in a classroom of three-year-olds! But I was appalled because when I heard my daughter repeat these words from her teacher, I wondered about times when she might be in danger from potential abusers, or even from future love interests who might want to try her boundaries. I caught a foretaste of her becoming the obedient girl that I was, and I had to wonder, what could be the alternative?

I can't quite recall what I did in that situation; I probably wrote a panicky email to the daycare director, who probably responded graciously. She likely proposed some more palatable alternatives to the robotic response proposed by the teacher and indicated how the school was teaching about healthy boundaries. Problem solved, small scale.

But a larger-scale problem is in play here. We're trained to think of "no" as a bad or negatively limiting word. We're trained to feel that boundaries are punitive. They can be especially scary to set when we have a history of people hurting us. Women who set boundaries sexually are "frigid" or worse; men who set boundaries about what they want to happen with their bodies are "unmasculine." The payoff is that with boundaries, everyone seems to lose. But it doesn't have to be this way. With boundaries, we can all win. And there are good biblical precedents for setting boundaries.

From the first pages of Scripture, we worship a God who sets boundaries. Genesis 1 is all about creating order out of chaos. Light from darkness; land from sea; different types of animals; male and female humans. Many of the writings of Genesis and elsewhere in the Torah have a strong sense of division. Part of God's nature is to bring creation into alignment through realization of different types of categories.

For the ancient Israelites, delineating things into "clean" and "unclean" categories helped them preserve a special sense of identity in a world where they were outnumbered and overpowered by a great number of other peoples. Rather than the things they categorized necessarily being all good or all bad in every case, it was a matter of staying within the sacred identity that the Israelites defined for themselves, through abiding by rules about blended fibers or dietary restrictions. Anthropologist Mary Douglas in her text *Purity and Danger* explores how the dietary laws and other customs laid out in the Old Testament demonstrate this need to keep separate what might identify Israelites with outsiders while also keeping them holy to God. What is "defiling" isn't objectively dirty, but only dirty through a distinction from something else. Douglas writes:

> If we can abstract pathogenicity and hygiene from our notion of dirt, we are left with the old definition of dirt as matter out of place. This is a very suggestive approach. It implies two conditions: a set of ordered relations and a contravention of that order. Dirt then, is never a unique, isolated event. Where there is dirt there is a system. Dirt is the by-product of a systematic ordering and classification of matter, in so far as ordering involves rejecting inappropriate elements.[1]

It isn't that dirt is bad, or that stuff besides dirt is inherently good, but making distinctions and drawing boundaries gives a sense of who and whose we are. Drawing lines and boundaries can lead to exclusion. But, used rightly, boundaries empower us and those around us.

In the New Testament, even with the advent of Jesus and the new Christian understandings of how his miraculous life, death, and resurrection fulfilled Old Testament prophecies, this idea of being "set apart" remained. For example, 1 Peter 2:9–12 reads:

> But you are a chosen people, a royal priesthood, a holy nation, God's own people, in order that you may proclaim the excellence of him who called you out of darkness into his marvelous light.
>
> Once you were not a people,
> but now you are God's people;
> once you had not received mercy,
> but now you have received mercy.
>
> Beloved, I urge you as aliens and exiles to abstain from the desires of the flesh that wage war against the soul. Conduct yourselves honorably among the gentiles, so that, though they malign you as evildoers, they may see your honorable deeds and glorify God when he comes to judge. (1 Peter 2:9–12)

We are aliens even in our own homelands, set apart through this sense that God has called us in his mercy, called us out of shadow and into light. There are borders and boundaries that make us aliens and exiles. The boundaries that keep us in bondage are not harsh laws and restrictive dictates, but a sense of our belovedness and belonging to the One who has called us.

The things that identify us lead us to set boundaries that maintain our distinctiveness as those who are holy and chosen by God. This is not a curse but a blessing. Like the Israelites, like the early church, we can proclaim our belonging to God through the totality of how we live.

Part of boundaries involves honoring who we know ourselves to be. Knowing ourselves well is the first step to being able to have healthy sexual relationships with anyone, including ourselves! Once again, Jesus says, "And a second is like it: You shall love your neighbor *as yourself*" (Matthew 22:39, emphasis mine). In knowing ourselves as sexual beings, we cannot really love ourselves without practicing good sexual boundaries. Particularly for women, the overwhelming focus of sexuality can be giving ourselves to others. And self-giving is what sex is supposed to be about, so that's not a misplaced thought! But giving of ourselves sexually simply to make people love us is subtly different from mutually sharing ourselves—and it's unhealthy. Sex is not supposed to be a way to earn love! Sex does not make us worthy! We need boundaries around sexuality to be sure that we are sharing ourselves sexually not in any kind of transactional agreement, but as a free and just self-giving that is mutually shared.

Boundaries, in other words, are a way of saying: "I love my neighbor as myself. I love myself enough to say no, even though saying no may be awkward or uncomfortable. I can say no because I know what I'm saying yes to, as well. I matter as much as my partner, or as much as whomever the person making requests matters."

Boundaries should mean that sexual activity doesn't become transactional for any of us. Sex shouldn't be traded for what approximates love to vulnerable people. Too often, we can feel unworthy unless we're offering people access to the most vulnerable parts of ourselves. Too often, we're taught that we won't be valued unless we have sexual interactions with others. Nobody should feel that they must offer up their bodies in order to meet their basic needs. Boundaries mean that we know we don't need to use sex to get something else.

Hopefully we all know by now that sexuality requires mutual consent. We should be deeply mindful of what a violation it is when someone overlooks our no or even our lack of enthusiasm and goes ahead with sexual activity anyway. Sexual violence remains a huge problem, and we'll consider it in more detail in the next chapter.

Since setting boundaries is tough for a lot of us, especially women and girls who have been socialized to be agreeable, I think it's worth brainstorming ways that we can practice having good boundaries. Here are a few of my ideas:

1. Overcommunicating is not always a bad thing! I think that thinking and talking with a partner before the heat of the moment is helpful. Anyway, communication and conversation are really sexy! What good partner *doesn't* want to know how to make their partner feel safe, connected, and respected? If a partner isn't open to hearing about your boundaries and sharing about theirs, that may be a red flag. Talking about boundaries doesn't need to look like a threat: "Do this and I will leave." It can communicate kindness and respect for one's partner and for oneself: "In this relationship, I'm looking to respect myself and you by doing X, Y, and Z," or maybe "I know myself, and I need to avoid X, Y, and Z. Is that something you think you can support me in?" Ideally, this is not an ultimatum, but an invitation to even more communication. I do think there's a time and place for ultimatums where issues of health and safety are concerned, but ideally, such conversations take place in the context of a healthy partnership!

2. It's a good idea to set boundaries, for oneself and as couples, outside of the context in which things might get hot and heavy. In the moment, a well-considered choice about boundaries can feel daunting. Saying no for the first time in a situation of physical intimacy can be swayed easily by the emotions and sensations of the moment, the desire to be a "good" partner, and the fear of letting someone else or ourselves down.

3. Boundaries don't exist at the expense of relationships. Boundaries create relationship. It's easy to think that when we set boundaries, we are limiting the possibility for relationship, and most of us don't want to do that! But boundaries give relationships shape and definition. It's a courtesy and a gift to one's partner to let them know where the space is in which a relationship can flourish and be well. Without boundaries, relationships are like an invasive species of plant, like kudzu; they can run all over the place and get out of hand. Nobody wants a yard full of kudzu. But everyone loves a beautiful, flourishing garden where there's space for all the flowers and plants to receive sunlight, rain, and the nutrients of the soil. In the Song of Songs, when the lovers speak to each other, the imagery of gardens predominates: "I come to my garden, my sister, my bride" (Song of Songs 5:1). First, the garden is *mine*. I have the right to choose what grows there and what does not belong. This is true regardless of gender and marital status. It's a place for our enjoyment and pleasure. Second, the garden is a place of beauty and cultivation. The garden is for flourishing and growth, and what cuts off that growth can be removed.

4. Boundaries help protect the integrity of the relationship. Our boundaries are not simply for within the relationship, but to guard it against infidelity that threatens to destroy the relationship. Continuing with the garden imagery, the most beautiful blossoms open in private. Extolling the female lover, the male lover says, "A garden locked is my sister, my bride, a garden locked, a fountain sealed" (Song of Songs 4:12). Relationships can flourish when the intimacy within them is unique. Scripture values sexual fidelity immensely. While we can easily criticize the patriarchs of the Old Testament for having multiple wives or taking enslaved women to bear them children (and yes, this criticism is valid), the movement of Scripture is toward singular sexual relationships between partners. This is partially because of what marriage represents: a covenantal bond that uniquely ties together one entity (God) with another (Israel or the church). Covenants originated in treaties between nations. Scripture recounts how covenants become deeply theological and personal as, first, God forges them with humanity, and then, humans echo that relational bond. We profess and celebrate our belief in the marital covenant union as it points us back to the unique relationship between Christ and the church.

5. **In marriage, fidelity is expected.** But in dating, things can be a little murkier, especially before the relationship is committed. In my millennial generation, we use the term DTR—defining the relationship—conversation; I'm not sure how young folks of Generation Z or beyond articulate this phenomenon! I think it's a great idea to be open to dates with multiple people early in the dating process, with a lot of physical limits involved. But it's important that both people are on the same page. When two dating people decide to be exclusive, it's important that there's conversation about what this is going to mean! What counts as "cheating"? Where do the lines of

physical and emotional fidelity begin and end? Especially in my experiences of dating in my thirties, I've realized that not everybody shares the same understandings, especially when we cross cultures.

6. Boundaries are important whether we're dating, in other forms of romantic relationships, or married! It's an unfortunate myth that once wedlock is sealed, all bets are off and anything goes. If anything, a lifelong partnership requires *more* intentionality about how boundaries are practiced and tended. If marriage is for the growth in holiness and wellness of each party—in other words, their mutual flourishing—then each partner needs to be focused on honoring the other's boundaries. This is true even and especially when we take seriously Paul's words in 1 Corinthians that a married couple should not withhold themselves except for a specified time and agreement. Paul foresees times in which there's a need for abstinence or reshaping what married relationships look like. If we're in it for the long haul—which, short of catastrophic, potentially relationship-ending behavior like abuse or infidelity, I certainly hope we are—then we need to make sure that our sexual relationship with our spouse honors their needs and values immensely.

All these characteristics of boundaries refocus us on loving God and loving neighbor. Boundaries structure the ways we're able to love our neighbor while fully loving ourselves, too. We've all experienced too much of a good thing in one way or another, whether it was a hot fudge sundae where overzealous application of hot fudge overflowed the dish or a significant other who took a good night kiss a little too far. We've probably also experienced being gut-checked ourselves when somebody else expressed a boundary to us. How we respond to others' boundaries matters, as well. Recently, I asked a coworker what she'd be doing if she wasn't employed at our workplace, and she kindly let me know that wasn't something she wanted to discuss with me, her friend from work. Since then, I've been much more mindful of my questions to her, remembering that our friendship comes with the added layer that we work together in a professional context. Her answer to my question helped me grow in response to a boundary.

Boundary setting is for everybody. Women can and should set boundaries. Men can and should set boundaries. When we receive boundaries, when someone trusts us enough to share a boundary, we can respond with "Thank you!" Because sharing boundaries involves sharing about our deep needs, insecurities, fears, and wishes, when we find the voice to express and share with a partner where they stop and we begin, that's a gift. Sexual abuse, misconduct, and assault can easily happen, not most commonly from an archvillain or a creepily hooded stranger, but from people we also know and love. And maybe even from ourselves.

Having good boundaries around power dynamics is crucial. We should *all* have age-related boundaries to help keep children and youth safe, and boundaries about involvement with people who are subordinate to us as adults (bosses and employees, professors and students, pastors and congregants, etc.). People who are under our power in one way or another just aren't available as potential romantic partners. When somebody needs our approval to get from point A to point B, the ability to freely consent is simply not present. Possibly, after roles change, it *might* become appropriate to have an intimate relationship, but not when the hierarchical relationship exists. Both as the "supervisor" and the "staff" in this situation (though, granted, there are many different configurations to this situation), we need to be mindful that a relationship may not be as innocent as all romantic relationships feel in their honeymoon phase.

Jesus teaches us clarity in boundaries as a virtue of a faithful follower. In speaking of oaths, Jesus says, "Let your word be 'Yes, Yes' or 'No, No'; anything more than this comes from the evil one" (Matthew 5:37). There's something beautifully simple about this clarity. We don't owe just anyone an explanation of our commitments that we make with intimacy. Our yeses and nos can be firm and direct; embellishment is not necessary, and the expectation that it is can be of Satan. While this might feel a little dramatic in the context of physical intimacy, I think it applies. So many of us are socialized to believe that we must apologize for or justify the choices we make sexually, especially when it comes to abstinence. But our yes or our no is enough! Jesus' words can empower us to set boundaries with confidence, knowing that we owe the reasons for them to nobody but God.

Granted, in significant relationships, we probably want to provide a little more context when explaining our values and commitments. For those whom we truly love, it makes sense to invest in helping them understand why we do what we do. It is also is crucial to listen to what our partner wants to express as well. Commitments and values can often be developed together within a relationship. But this kind of communication is something that's earned through trust over time. We don't owe anybody an explanation for who we are or what we do. I tend to have a strong distaste for financial metaphors, but if every act that builds trust makes a deposit, we're going to need a lot of deposits in our relationship banks before a big withdrawal is made. Explaining boundaries can be a big withdrawal, and Billy Jean from down the street whom we barely know doesn't have that much in the bank yet. Our deepest needs of privacy, space, and intimacy—and how those work as boundaries—aren't ever something we owe the general public an explanation for.

Loving our neighbors means listening to their boundaries. Loving our neighbors *authentically* means voicing our own boundaries, too. Loving ourselves also means honoring our boundaries. Boundaries are a way to build in love together the dwelling place of our fragile and beautiful temples, our bodies, on a foundation that feels steady and safe.

6

When Things Don't Go Right

SEXUAL PROBLEMS

Sexuality is a beautiful gift from God. And it seems like it should be such a simple thing to sexually relate to a committed partner, right? But it isn't always. There's a lot that can intervene in what can in fantasy be such a natural way to connect. Sexual dysfunction isn't talked about much in most Christian circles. I'm not a sex therapist, and I'm not going to postulate on how we fix these types of dysfunctions, so please see a licensed sex therapist for that! There are good ones out there. But what I can do is encourage us to talk more openly about these issues, while considering the wisdom of Scripture and especially of the great commandment.

Writing this chapter wasn't originally in my plan for this book. After writing a couple of books about trauma, I was fully committed to writing a happy book about sexuality—because sexuality has by and large been a joyous and healing experience for me. But it didn't feel right to sign off on this work while not addressing the flatulent hippopotamus in the room—which is that sexuality is *not* always easy or happy.

I'll never forget when one of my students, reading the Song of Songs, shared that it was more difficult for them to read this material than some of the more painful stories in the Old Testament about sexuality. Why? Because it presented an idyllic image of sexuality that was mutual, vibrant, and healing, and that just wasn't how they had experienced sexuality in their life. It felt invalidating to read all that idyllic and beautiful material without a full acknowledgement of how difficult it can be to share ourselves sexually with another person. And if this feels like your story as well, I want you to know that I hear you and see you. Your journey with sexual intimacy and pain matters. Intimacy and pain are an integral part of God's story, and you are not alone.

There's an almost endless array of ways that we can experience sexual dysfunction in our relationships. I want to talk more specifically about a few that I've heard come up in many conversations—specifically, traumatic pasts, the shame we can feel about engaging sexually with someone after long seasons of abstinence, issues with sexual function, and infidelity of various kinds. Most importantly, as we navigate these issues, we're still trying to balance and navigate the crucial components of love of God, self, and other.

There's so much more to be said about each of these topics. I offer my reflections on these topics not as a claim that these are the exhaustive words of wisdom, but as a sticky note that *far* more conversation is needed, and that the resources of the church can and should be helping us out a lot more than what we've experienced.

TRAUMA

An astounding number of people of all genders are carrying trauma of all kinds, including sexual. Among certain populations, like the chronically homeless folks that I work with, we assume that all people have trauma. When I speak to groups of people about intimate partner violence and the Bible, I always assume that there are survivors in the room, which is a good practice, because it turns out, there always are.

When abuse happens within a relationship, sex can change. What might previously have come across as intimate can now feel threatening. This is something that I experienced during my drawn-out process of trying to leave a violent relationship. In this period, we were still physically involved. The abuse I experienced was not sexual, but it colored my experience of all our interactions. At the same time, though the relationship was dangerous and I knew, intellectually, that I needed to exit the marriage, I struggled to extract myself from the relationship in part because it was my first intimate partnership. All of this is a testament to how abuse ruptures relationship and causes layers of harm and confusion.

All of this is compounded when abuse is explicitly sexual. Many people who have waited until marriage to choose to share in sexual interaction may have experienced sexual abuse in their past. This may not even be disclosed before or at the beginning of marriage, especially for male survivors, who may fear that their partner's or others' perceptions of their masculinity is at stake. Others may have tried to disclose to trusted others, only to find their trust betrayed by poor responses to sharing confidential information. Others may be carrying the pain of feeling that church teachings of abstinence-only sex education mean that they're stained or deflowered in some terrible way by their experiences of trauma. Sexual violence is terrible, and yet no aspect of our history can increase or decrease our value. We are, as we are and with all that we are carrying, beloved and enough.

For most people who experience abuse, the abuse will have happened not "out there," by some stranger with proverbial cloak and dagger, but at the hands of someone known.[1] Being abused by a trusted person can make what was familiar feel unsafe. As I've written about elsewhere, this is not a "women's problem." This is a burden carried by men and women and children, people of every sexual identity and gender, and people from every walk of life.

When we have experienced sexual trauma, sexual intimacy with even a trusted partner can feel extremely activating. The body can remember what it experienced, how it was violated, and even the smallest touches can generate a flashback. All of this can make sex, at best, not sexually interesting, and at worst, painful and retraumatizing. These are situations where professional help is crucial.

Healing can occur in many ways, including through therapeutic and psychiatric intervention. But it also happens in relationships. Just as so much damage and pain occur in relationships, healing and grace can be sacramentally imparted through relationships, too. In marriage and committed relationships, we make the promise to bear witness to each other's life stories in the fullest way we know. We, like Thomas in the gospel of John, dare to approach and touch each other's wounds, not as voyeurs, but as disciples to the Christ who was wounded first. And finding these wounds concealed on one another, we can exclaim, like Thomas, "My Lord and my God!" (John 20:28) as we again encounter the crucified Christ even in the fragile and resilient body of our partner.

And we, the ones whose wounds become revealed, slowly over time, experience healing as we realize our wounds are not too much for our beloved, whether that's a trusted lover or God. They're not so much that we can no longer share Christ.

Our wounds are worthy of gentle touch, and they're worthy of healing. There's no need for shame when we know that we can receive the touch of love even here.

SHAME

Shame is the shadow side to our thinking about sexuality. So many of us are taught to be afraid of our own bodies. So many of us believe, even if not consciously, that our desires are bad. So many of us carry the weight of feeling like our pasts make us less than we truly are. And, sadly, this can be true whether our pasts are something chosen or something done to us.

It would be easy to say: Just don't feel that way. Don't carry with you what Jesus carries for you. Release the pain and the shame and everything else along with it.

It would be easy to say, and probably there's some truth in that, but there's also a lot that's wrong with it. Because shame isn't like waste removal Tuesdays in my neighborhood. We don't just set our junk out on the curb and count on it being taken away. Shame is slimy and sneaky. Sure, the gospel removes shame, but how do we get to that blessed place of shame-free existence?

It's common pop psychology knowledge these days that shame and guilt are related but not identical. I had a nondenominational pastor in my twenties who used to say all the time, "Guilt means I did something bad; shame means I am something bad," channeling Brené Brown. And I think that tracks. Shame tells us that we are not worthy to be in the presence of God or one another. Shame tells us that we should be hiding instead.

Many of us who grew up in purity culture are so conditioned to think of anything sexually related as shameful that it's hard to release even when we are married or in a committed relationship. It's hard for many of us to get to the point of accepting that our sexuality is part of our God-created design. For those who grew up in a context with a strong or exclusive emphasis on abstinence before marriage, it can be a huge jump to go from being completely closed off to sexual interactions with others to sharing ourselves in the most intimate way. How *can* we be open to shared intimacy with our partner when all this time, we've been saving ourselves for something?

For those affected by this aspect of purity culture, it's important to remember that our sexual selves are part of the way that God created us. It is not shameful to carry out these acts with a loved one. It is not sinful to join ourselves together to share pleasure, creativity, and passion. It might take us a while to feel fully comfortable expressing ourselves openly with a partner, and that is perfectly reasonable.

SEXUAL DYSFUNCTION

Often, shame is so strongly experienced in relationship that it can become one of the intertwined issues leading toward sexual dysfunction. Sometimes, the shame we've internalized manifests emotionally, with withdrawal, anxiety, or depression. Some people, especially when they're going through transitions in relationships like their first sexual encounters, may experience it in more physical ways. Men can experience erectile dysfunction or problems with orgasm. Women can experience pain with penetration (or pain that prevents penetration or other intimacy) or an inability to orgasm. I think that these problems are far too uncommonly talked about for Christian couples. I've been around the rodeo a few times now. In different church settings that prize abstinence before marriage, I've heard women behind closed doors with other women sharing issues that they or their husbands were having, marring what they thought should have been the honeymoon period in their relationships.

From these secluded women's group conversations, I've learned this: When we *do* have problems sexually, they can easily compound themselves because we can get so focused on whatever the problem is. It can become all-consuming in the relationship, blocking out whatever is going well. Both men and women can feel humiliated that this is a problem that they are having. Even if a partner reaches out compassionately, being willing to work things out, it's not an easy thing to share. Both men and women can feel like their entire sexual identities are called into question by what they perceive as their inability to please their partner.

Sometimes, physical and emotional problems in relationships are so severe that penetrative or other forms of sex aren't possible. This can occur for both men and women! There can be manifold reasons for dysfunction, and I'm not trying to single out shame or anxiety as the only ones. Whatever the reasons we experience these issues, *we* are worth pausing and examining what's at their root. Our sense of identity can be so enmeshed in our sexuality that feeling like ourselves—like a full, competent adult and a worthy partner—can seem really tough when we are struggling so much.

Difficult emotions around sexual struggles make sense, and they come from a good place, I think. We *want* to please our partners. We *want* to satisfy their expectations and make all their dreams come true. (Right?) We want to be the person they think we are. We can feel inadequate and alone, and the last person we want to talk to about what we're experiencing may be our partner, whom we feel like we're letting down. We start overthinking and becoming more and more anxious, and then, it turns out, we've overthought so much that the original problem feels way harder to overcome than before. We have even more trouble becoming aroused. We have even more trouble being vulnerable. We have even more trouble achieving orgasm or other physical pleasure.

So often, we frame sex as a performance and achievement. We understand sex as something that has to be "performed," especially for men. We talk about "achieving" orgasms like it puts us on an Olympic podium. But maybe part of the problem lies in this wording. Maybe we're dealing with an issue not just of individuals' organs not working quite the way we think they should, but of a societal sexual dysfunction. And I don't think the two—individual dysfunction and societal dysfunction—are disconnected, either.

Our society is dysfunctional in its insistence that we get sexual worth in all the wrong ways. We're supposed to get it through conquest, through flawless bodies, through many partners—or conversely, through virginity. But that's not really what "good" sex is about at all. Sure, in what some or even many heterosexual couples understand as traditional marriage, the husband takes a more active role in initiating penetration. This is what's understood primarily as a man's performance, while a woman's "performance" is to be receptive to the man or sometimes to "achieve" orgasm. The metric of intercourse's success is often the man's pleasure and orgasm. In a more egalitarian society, success might be the woman's orgasm, too.

But why is this language of performance and achievement so common? The values here seem upside down. It puts a heavy burden on the participants of the intimacy to get things right. Such a burden can create a high-stress environment for all parties. And stress and sexual satisfaction simply do not go together, as any two parents trying to have closeness in the bedroom while also struggling with getting a baby or toddler to sleep understand all too well. Things tend to go in the opposite direction when stress is involved, compounding the sense of failure. There's also the temptation on both sides to react badly when things don't go as planned.

So maybe it's time to reframe our language around these things. Maybe we need to realize that we work together to empower and facilitate the greatest act of intimacy of humankind. Maybe orgasm isn't a thing to be "achieved" but a thing to be "built" together, each person adding something to the other's efforts to fulfill the full job of total embrace. Both partners are part of this building for each other. Nobody needs to feel like they're carrying the weight of the world to make it happen. It's a journey that we take together so that everyone experiences the ecstasy of what it is to be fully known and loved.

When we enter marriage or other committed relationships, we're also in the journey for the long haul. Who we are one year is not going to be the same another year. Natural aging, as well as accidents, injuries, pregnancy, childbirth, sleep deprivation, and stress all influence the way that we are present sexually in our relationship. Being postpartum often means that women simply don't feel like they have the energy to devote to sex as well as facing problems like prolapse or tearing, and breastfeeding or lack of sleep decreasing sex drives. Perimenopause and menopause in women bring hormonal changes that affect their libido. Men can experience declining testosterone over time. Honestly, when we get married, we're not signing up to be committed to one person over a lifetime, but one partner who is going to manifest in many ways as we mature, age, and shift as time goes on.

When we say our marriage vows, we aren't signing up for guaranteed sexual access and satisfaction. That would be a pretty shallow version of marriage. I wasn't mature enough to understand that fully when I first got married. If I could change one thing from early in my first marriage, it would be to respond with grace and love when we faced struggles and to assure my partner that my love wasn't conditional on how well things were going in bed. Our partners need to know they have our support when we journey through sexual challenges together, so long as those challenges don't involve unsafety or abuse of any kind, including physical, emotional, or sexual.

INFIDELITY

I haven't personally experienced the pain of infidelity. Unlike many other topics that I've written about, I don't know how it feels to have a partner betray me in this way. However, I do know that infidelity breaks relationships. Sometimes, they're reparable, but most of the time, I believe they're not. Infidelity breaks relationships in such a way that dissolution becomes likely, and perhaps inevitable.

One of the biggest mistakes I believe that the church often makes when it talks about infidelity is to claim that somehow the abandoned partner is to be blamed. This is especially common when the dynamic involves a husband cheating on his wife. The wife is typically blamed for not having sexually satisfied the man enough, or for being too "manly" and thus pushing her husband away. (When a woman cheats, she's much more likely to be written off as a fallen woman or a tempter of men, with no or little blame laid at the man's feet.)

The Bible treats infidelity seriously—seriously enough that Jesus makes special mention of it as a legitimate reason for divorce. (I am not saying that infidelity should be regarded as the *only* acceptable reason for divorce; I have plenty of background from my personal journey that I should hope Jesus would be understanding of.) We considered part of this text in an earlier chapter:

> "You have heard that it was said, "You shall not commit adultery,'" Jesus declares. But I say to you that everyone who looks at a woman with lust has already committed adultery with her in his heart. If your right eye causes you to sin, tear it out and throw it away; it is better for you to lose one of your members than for your whole body to be thrown into hell. And if your right hand causes you to sin, cut it off and throw it away; it is better for you to lose one of your members than for your whole body to go into hell.
>
> It was also said, "Whoever divorces his wife, let him give her a certificate of divorce." But I say to you that anyone who divorces his wife, except on the ground of sexual immorality, causes her to commit adultery, and whoever marries a divorced woman commits adultery. (Matthew 5:27–32)

There's a lot to unpack here, maybe starting with how Jesus doesn't want men exploiting their wives when they get tired of them by divorcing them for no reason. In this context, limiting divorce to cases of adultery makes a lot of sense. Jesus didn't live in a world where women could file for divorce for all kinds of reasons, including abuse and infidelity. But we can also notice how Jesus, addressing an audience, it seems, of men (see how the text assumes that the woman is the object of lust?), *expands* the definition of what constitutes adultery. If looking with lust counts as infidelity—well, let's just say that probably made a lot of folks uncomfortable.

So I think Jesus would be very concerned about and sympathetic to the many people today who find themselves in marriages where there's sexual infidelity of various kinds, whether that's cheating or use of porn or inappropriate sexual behavior that destroys a marriage.

Please note, on this front: I think it's a big problem when a married pastor or other church leader—or really any person in a committed relationship—commits sexual misconduct and the community or leadership minimizes it as infidelity. Yes, it *is* infidelity, but it may also be something else, and it's important to call things as they are. We can't minimize the pain of a victim by focusing exclusively on the infidelity and neglecting to examine how it was also rape, abuse, misconduct, and so on. These crimes should have legal ramifications far more than simply removal from an office or role.

I believe that infidelity can include use of pornography. We've already talked about some of the ways that pornography can be harmful for the ways it turns people into mere objects for sexual desire. Within a marriage, what does it mean if we are turning to screens or other content for sexual gratification instead of looking to our spouse as the one we desire? Even if a couple views pornography together, I think it redirects attention and devotion from the beloved to the disconnected and abstract body of another person, their humanity set a screen's distance away. Pornography conditions us to experience attraction and desire as impersonal and disconnected from intimacy with a partner. It distorts sex from an act of love to a vending machine transaction, where the vending machine is the body of another child of God, stripped of that dignity. It dishonors the marriage to have that sort of transactional relationship, between a person and a screen, replace the beautiful dance of really knowing another person.

I'm not taking a stand here on whether repeated use of pornography qualifies as an addiction. I know many people in recovery from substance use, and I know beloved ones who have struggled or currently struggle with pornography use as well. I don't want those who struggle to hear my words as condemnation. I want all who struggle with pornography to know, as we *all* need to know, that God loves us first, that God is always reconciling us to him, and that healing and grace are not only possible but God's greatest gifts to each one of us.

Nor am I saying that every marriage should end because of an affair or pornography use. But I do know people who have been deeply wounded by their partner's sexual violence, affairs, or pornography usage. I do know many people for whom it's been impossible to continue a marriage after the profound betrayal of infidelity, and I would wager that is true for many other people. The blame lies not in the abandoned partner who perhaps files for divorce to sever the relationship, but in the infidelity itself for breaking the relationship.

Sexuality needs to be held both fiercely and tenderly in a relationship. It is one of the most intimate parts of ourselves we have to offer. I have a beautiful blown glass teapot ornament that I display at my house. It was given to me by someone who loved me. If I decided to share that ornament with someone else, and they hurled it on the ground in pieces, I would be devastated. The fact that this happened to me at the hands of a loved one makes it even worse. And I imagine that this is, on a small and symbolic scale, what infidelity from a committed partner feels like. We must, as partners, hold with tenderness the gift of self that our partners offer us. It's one of the greatest gifts we'll ever give or receive. How could we afford it less than with our highest honor, our greatest tenderness, and our most passionate care?

Sexuality is a journey that's best shared together with trust and communication. It's not a destination. With time, patience, communication, trust, and sometimes professional guidance, it's possible to create a relationship where partners can thrive. We're not guaranteed a voyage that is smooth or uneventful, but if we reorient ourselves to the great commandment—love of God, other, and self—we can find a way to navigate stormy waters. We can hold our partners with grace when they struggle with their sexuality in light of shame, trauma, physical challenges, or pain, and we can also warmly welcome support when we face our own sexual difficulties. At the same time, though, not all burdens are ones that we can hold. Sometimes, when our own efforts cannot fix them, we need to trust relationships into the love and care of God, even when that may mean relinquishing the relationship itself. We cannot neglect the love of self, without which love of others isn't even fully possible.

HEALING

Throughout the stories of the Gospels, Jesus engages with people in their brokenness. He could almost resemble an itinerant magician through his miraculous restorations of sight, demonic exorcisms, raising of the dead, rehabilitation of walking, and so on, but we know he is so much more than that. Jesus prescribes real healing, not merely a "cure." Don't get me wrong—cures are great. What wouldn't we give for more rapid cures of childhood (and adult) cancers, dementia, chronic conditions, and more? In a cure, the problem is basically annihilated. That's not necessarily what healing means. As a chaplain, I have seen people in stages of dying experience healing. I have seen people realize what was truly important in their lives, realize that they mattered to God and others, and reconcile with loved ones—only to die hours or days later. Cured? Nope. Healed? I think so, though only God knows a person's heart.

So many of us have so very much to heal from in the sexual arena, whether it's betrayals of loved ones, church teachings that caused great harm, or our own feelings about ourselves. Because sexuality is deep, intimate, and precious, wounds to it are particularly painful. As I've said before, there are many resources for different types of healing, and I absolutely believe that a therapist who specializes in sexual challenges and trauma can be an invaluable ally in our journeys of healing.

But there's no need to compartmentalize the psychological and the spiritual. Healing means finding peace with ourselves, others, and God, even with the most painful circumstances of our lives. Those three areas where we need peace are a mirror image of the areas where Jesus asks us to pour out our love. When we can experience love just as we offer it, when we have wellness in the ways we share ourselves, then we'll know what it's like to feel more whole.

Healing is hard won, often, and it doesn't necessarily mean that scars vanish. Let's remember, always, that our Lord was raised from the dead with his scars still on his body. We don't need to forget—nor can we—the places of pain. The sites of wounds, when slowly healed over time, can also become a source of great healing for the world. As a first-year college student, keeping a prayer journal in which I reflected on some of my own experiences of trauma, I wrote, "Lord, take these wounds, and in my bleeding, heal the world." Maybe I was wrong, then, that the healing of the world would come through my bleeding; more like Hemingway, I now believe that healing manifests in scars, road maps of pain and recovery, that we can point to and say with confidence, "This is what the Lord has done."

God gives us agency in healing. God does not force healing on anyone. In one of my favorite stories from the Old Testament, Naaman, the general of the Syrian army, is afflicted with a terrible skin disease. A young Israelite girl, whom Naaman presumably kidnapped after killing her parents, knows that the prophet Elisha has the power to enact God's healing. Elisha is indeed willing to give advice! But he denies Naaman a personal audience, and Naaman gets mad and at first refuses help. Then, when he finally hears the prophet's advice, Naaman is affronted that it seems so basic: Go take a bath seven times in the Jordan. This is devilishly simple, and Namaan feels his journey might have been a waste: "Are not Abana and Pharpar, the rivers of Damascus, better than all the waters of Israel? Could I not wash in them and be clean?" (2 Kings 5:12).

Naaman's assent to follow the advice is ultimately the only thing that helps him get better, but his healing requires him to reach the point where he's willing to cooperate, first. His subordinates must convince him to participate: "His servants approached and said to him, 'Father, if the prophet had commanded you to do something difficult, would you not have done it? How much more, when all he said to you was, "Wash, and be clean"?'" (2 Kings 5:13). Only after this urging does Naaman comply.

So often, healing is difficult to accept. Healing comes differently than we thought it would, and the process means we must grow in ways we didn't expect. Healing requires us to reach out and accept help we might feel too good for, and sometimes it means simply embracing God's mercy that lies beyond ourselves. We resist it, at times, because it doesn't feel fair to have to wander through a wilderness that we may not have placed ourselves in to begin with.

The choice to seek healing is still ours, though we might struggle to decide to do so. When Jesus encounters a blind man outside Jericho in the gospel of Mark, the man is crying out to him for help, but Jesus still asks him to articulate what he wants help with, what he wants to happen next:

> Jesus stood still and said, "Call him here." And they called the blind man, saying to him, "Take heart; get up, he is calling you." So throwing off his cloak, he sprang up and came to Jesus. Then Jesus said to him, "What do you want me to do for you?" The blind man said to him, "My teacher, let me see again." Jesus said to him, "Go; your faith has made you well." Immediately he regained his sight and followed him on the way. (Mark 10:49–52)

Jesus' question to the man might feel a little misplaced to us. Well, duh, Jesus, of *course* the man wants help restoring his vision! But to Jesus, disability isn't necessarily something that singles a person out for needing healing. Jesus instead wants to give the man agency in defining what he needs for himself. (This, by the way, is a beautiful model for caregiving. There's no need to assume we know what the other person needs. It's so much better to ask and empower a person in a moment when they may feel very vulnerable.) Here, the man *does* say his sight is the problem, but I'm sure that Jesus is still glad he checked; what if the man thought his spleen or something else needed help instead? While healing happens through God's grace, channeled incarnationally through Jesus, healing happens with the consent and involvement of the person who needs help in some way.

On another occasion, Jesus encounters a man lying by the pool of Beth-zatha, where he has long awaited healing yet is unable to reach the waters where relief is promised. But

Jesus does not at all take for granted what the man wants him to do:

> When Jesus saw him lying there and knew that he had been there a long time, he said to him, "Do you want to be made well?" The ill man answered him, "Sir, I have no one to put me into the pool when the water is stirred up, and while I am making my way someone else steps down ahead of me." Jesus said to him, "Stand up, take your mat and walk." At once the man was made well, and he took up his mat and began to walk. (John 5:6–9)

That question, "Do you want to be made well?", resounds with me. There have been times when, if I'm being honest, I didn't want to be made well, because taking up my mat and walking sounded like a heck of a lot of work. After all, the reason I or the man by the pool waiting for healing was there for so long was because of some individual or communal betrayal. The man *shouldn't have had to* be there that long waiting for a literal leg up to reach the waters. Nobody should be callously passed by like that, yet pull-yourself-up-by-your-bootstraps culture can put the onus on each of us to find healing by ourselves. The story from Luke 5:17–39 shows us that good friends help us to get to a place of healing. The friends of a man who is paralyzed lower him through the ceiling to Jesus, showing us that healing is not an individualistic endeavor at all. Thank God for the friends who chisel through barriers to lay our broken bodies at Jesus' feet! I've had a few of those friends in my life, and I hope you have as well.

But the friends probably would have struggled to lower that man through the room if he had been kicking, screaming, and pulling their hair, like a toddler refusing to get buckled into a car seat. The man had to have the wisdom to know he needed help, or at least not resist it. We need to have, like the man marooned by the pool for so long, the boldness to cry out to God, to articulate, like the blind man outside Jericho, what it is we need, to reach out for it, even if we can't take the first step or any other step on our own. Healing is something we experience in cooperation with God's ultimate power. Because a coerced healing sounds like the mouthful of amoxicillin that my four-year-old daughter is just waiting to spit out.

I wonder how, in different moments of our lives, we will respond to Jesus' question: "Do you want to be made well?" Working at a low-barrier homeless shelter, I've realized that "to be made well" involves incredible risk. Every day, I meet with people who are helpless to the illness of addiction to drugs or alcohol. They have lost family, friends, homes, jobs, pets, children, many of the basic things that have given their (or anyone's) lives purpose and meaning. Yet reaching out for healing is one of the most difficult things that any of them do. Going into treatment means facing the reality of how the illness of addiction has been destructive, down to their core, and most folks aren't ready to do that. Addiction has been the coping mechanism through which they've dealt with trauma, loss, abandonment, and other forms of illness. For others, they'll go to treatment and last for a bit, but not stay for the entire program; it's hard to stay in a place that's unfamiliar and not have your coping mechanism with you! For still others, they'll go into treatment and then return to the community from which they came, only to find that exposure to drugs brings them back into the same cycle of illness. For some, it may take a few cycles, but the change will be permanent.

Not all of us suffer from the illness of chemical dependency. But working closely with those who do, I've learned that those neighbors in addiction and recovery have much to teach the rest of us about our relationships with our illness, dysfunction, and healing. None of us are whole. None of us are perfect. Many of us are, in our own ways, enslaved to patterns of brokenness, and it takes more courage than anything else in life to own up to them and reach out for help.

So, if Jesus approached any one of us today and asked, "Do you want to be made well?," if we were super honest, we might walk away sad, like the rich young man whom Jesus told nothing was lacking except giving away his own hang-up—his wealth (see Matthew 19:16–22).

Thankfully, in every area of our lives, this is a question that Jesus keeps offering us, time and time again. In the arena of our sexual brokenness, whatever that may look like in our lives, Jesus' invitation is no different. We are always welcome to say yes to the ways God moves to restore us through the sacraments, the ministry of the church, the work of therapists and other medical professionals, the love of a partner and a community, and the power of prayer. God is still speaking and still moving.

I wager that more of us than not have experienced the crippling shame and fear of some problem within our sexuality. There are few things more isolating than a problem in this area, because of the stigma so often attached to dealing with these types of issues. We can feel like no one in the world is available to be present to this type of pain. But we are not alone.

All of us deserve a community of people to support us. But even if people fail to do so, we have the promise of Scripture to guide us. One of the most poignant promises to me in the whole Bible is Psalm 23—which, by the way, is good for a lot more than funerals. In the beautiful, poetic words of the psalm of the King James Version of the Bible, "Yea, though I walk through the valley of the shadow of death, I will fear no evil:

for thou art with me; thy rod and thy staff they comfort me." It's not that we are spared walking through the valley of the shadow of death, but *when* we walk through the valley of the shadow of death, God is nearer to us than our own breath. Even though this journey of healing may take us down the darkest paths we've ever walked, through the darkest nights of the soul, our Shepherd will not leave us. Never. Ever.

7

Embracing Pleasure

THE GOOD OF THE BELOVED

Among my friends who saved sex until marriage, especially for religious reasons, like I did in my twenties, there can be a learning curve when it comes to experiencing pleasure as a couple or individually. It's quite something to go from a mindset of "most kinds of physical intimacy are unacceptable" to sharing one's body with another person while naked, and further, to feel good about doing it. Both men and women can struggle with this, especially when pleasure has been associated with sin.

I think a few different things are true at the same time when it comes to biblical sex. The point of sex in the Bible definitely is not pleasure, per se. Reproduction is the focus of more references to sex than pleasure is in the Bible, simply because it's so dang important to keep reproducing to (1) keep the culture alive, (2) continue family lines and make sure fathers had somebody to preserve their heritage and pass down their worldly inheritance to, and (3) ensure that there was help to do the significant amount of labor necessary for life within a largely agrarian society.

However, the Bible doesn't neglect pleasure as a component of sex. Even in the same breath as discussing the unlikely chance that she'll actually get to have a baby, Sarah seems to refer to sexual pleasure: "Shall I have pleasure, now that I am old and my husband has grown old?" (my translation of Genesis 18:12). Interestingly, the NRSVue translation as well as others veer away from the more literal reference to sexual pleasure, as Sarah's remarks might seem a little improper or uncomfortable. These translations prefer to have Sarah ask if she will have a *son*. Now, having a son is great and would make Sarah happy, but the word in Hebrew is *'ednah*, literally, for pleasure. We shouldn't reduce Sarah's response to merely the joy of childbirth, since the text suggests that her sensuality is also involved. What's so wrong about Sarah having some pleasure with her husband? Only our cultural barriers to pleasure, that's what.

The truth is, we can *all* be uncomfortable with embracing the reality that we're sexual beings. That includes old women like Sarah, apparently! There's no escaping the fact that sexuality, even in the Bible, is closely linked to the physical experience of pleasure.

It's also inescapable in the Bible that pleasure can lead us in the wrong direction, away from godly desires for our relationship and toward what biblical authors would deem unacceptable pleasures. For Paul in Romans, this includes behavior that breaks down socially acceptable patterns of relationship:

> Therefore God gave them over in the desires of their hearts to impurity, to the dishonoring of their bodies among

> themselves. They exchanged the truth about God for a lie and worshiped and served the creature rather than the Creator, who is blessed forever! Amen.
>
> For this reason God gave them over to dishonorable passions. Their females exchanged natural intercourse for unnatural, and in the same way also the males, giving up natural intercourse with females, were consumed with their passionate desires for one another. Males committed shameless acts with males and received in their own persons the due penalty for their error. (Romans 1:24–27)

We can say with assurance that Christians of good faith in every tradition disagree about the proper interpretation of verses regarding same-sex activities and relationships in the Bible. But rather than focusing on Paul's condemnation of same-sex sexual activities here, I am far more interested in considering how the root problem that Paul is confronting isn't pleasure but rather how improper worship of God and missing devotion to God results in failing to have proper reverence in our sexual passions. The implication may be that when we revere God appropriately, we will be able to have right relationship with one another too. Passion itself, even for Paul, is not the problem! It's neglecting to allow our passions to flow out of worship of God.

We can gather that when we worship God fully, our sexual relationships, including experiencing pleasure, can continue the worship of God that we've already begun. And this makes sense for those of us who've had the beautiful opportunity to experience covenantal intimacy with a spouse. Even some wedding vows reflect this reality. The Anglican Book of Common Prayer includes within its marriage vows the line "With my body I thee worship."[1] Taken at face value, we Christians might look askance at this. After all, we're only supposed to worship God, right?

But these marriage vows suggest something quite different from idolatry. The writers of the Anglican prayer book certainly don't intend for us to exchange worship of God for worship of our marriage partner! Instead, in saying, "With my body I thee worship," the liturgy intends for us to be so deeply invested in God that *even the sexual intimacy and pleasure that we experience with a partner* are an extension of that worship. Living life in love with God, we cannot help but know God deeper and adore him more when we experience his love through our partner.

Of all the books in the Bible, the Song of Songs most explicitly embraces and acknowledges sexual pleasure. What's more, the Song of Songs acknowledges that women experience sexual pleasure too. This probably doesn't sound very revelatory, as hopefully every reader of this book is aware that women have sexual pleasure as much as men, but this hasn't always been a concept that's taken for granted. In the Bible, often sex is talked about purely from a man's perspective. Men want sex, initiate sex, and take pleasure in sex in ways that women simply do not in most of Scripture.

However, the Song of Songs is unique because it celebrates sex in a way that at least appears to be written from a woman's perspective. Though the narrative voice of the Song does shift back and forth a bit, the lion's share of it seems to be written from the vantage point of the female lover talking to the male lover. She is particularly open about her own desire for the man.

All of this desire also *appears* to be out of the context of marriage. At the very least, marriage isn't talked about a whole lot, aside from the marriage of Solomon. After all, traditionally the Song of Songs has been said to be written by Solomon, that most lusty of all the kings of Israel with his many foreign wives (gasp). I don't really know whether Solomon wrote the Song of Songs, but I do know that whoever wrote it had a pretty good understanding of women's sexuality.

That's not to say that it's all sunlight and rainbows when we read the Song of Songs. Being a woman is tough, whether in the ancient world or today. The female character of the Song of Songs goes out in search of her male lover, and she is stripped and beaten. She adjures her handmaidens not to awaken love before it is ready—a solemn warning in an otherwise lighthearted account. Sometimes, the Song of Songs has been called a "feminist paradise," and I don't think it's that, exactly, but it's definitely a window into a much more female-involved sexuality than we see in many other places in Scripture.

The Song of Songs is forthright about pleasure being part of sexuality, for both men and women. While much of the entire book deals with the human body, chapter 5 vividly describes in thinly veiled metaphors how the female lover experiences sex. Speaking from a woman's perspective, the text reads:

> I was sleeping, but my heart was awake.
> The sound of my beloved knocking!
> "Open to me, my sister, my love,
>   my dove, my perfect one,
> for my head is wet with dew,
>   my locks with the drops of the night."
> I had put off my garment;
>   how could I put it on again?
> I had bathed my feet;
>   how could I soil them?

My beloved thrust his hand into the opening,
    and my inmost being yearned for him.
I arose to open to my beloved,
    and my hands dripped with myrrh,
my fingers with liquid myrrh,
    upon the handles of the bolt. (Song of Songs 5:2–5)

This passage is fascinating to me because, as much as women appear to be sexually objectified in much of the Bible, here they are present as sexual actors. They have their own desires, too. First off, this passage seems like it could be part of a dream sequence for the female lover. She is "sleeping," though her heart is still roving around with a healthy imagination. The beloved comes to her in her dream to engage her in passionate foreplay. Not jumping into full sexual intercourse, the beloved "thrusts his hand into the opening," still playing with the metaphor of the door, while also being more than a little suggestive of what types of foreplay are taking place.

Penetrative sex isn't what the lovers jump to, as this is a consensual and pleasurable interaction for both parties. It seems that the male lover, "thrusting his hand into the opening," seeks to arouse the female lover by using his hand to stimulate her before anything else takes place. And his efforts are not in vain! The woman responds with yearning. His time and attention mean that the woman is even more desirous of sharing herself with him, and sex will be more pleasurable for her. Presumably this satisfaction will benefit him also.

True to the physiological realities of many women, she responds to connection and touch. The "myrrh" that the woman is speaking of seems to reference the physiology of women's arousal, producing natural lubrication. The woman's arousal is not merely responsive here, either: she "arises" to open to the beloved. Her willing and enthusiastic participation, which should be the condition for consent in any circumstance of sexual interaction, is a major component of the narrative.

This sequence is extremely powerful. It demonstrates that in a healthy interaction, pleasure is not simply the province of men, but something that should be shared between a couple. The woman "opens" when she is ready, when there's plenty of "myrrh" to be had. She wants it. She's ready for it. And that's okay—in fact, that's good!

While the Bible has a mixed record on the consensual nature of sexual interactions, I'm grateful that this example of mutual enjoyment is here to set the record straight about God's desires for us. Contrary to what so many of us were taught, sex isn't just or even mainly about male ejaculation. Sex is about *shared* enjoyment. I risk emphasizing this again because I've encountered plenty of people for whom that hasn't been true. I've heard women that I've known well say things like, "Sex is really for men. Sex isn't really all that enjoyable for women. I've never even had an orgasm."

The Song of Songs stands squarely in the way of this thinking. For a majority of the book, a *woman* is speaking, extolling the virtues and attractiveness of the male lover. She wants sex. She goes out to seek it. She welcomes it when it comes to her. She risks much for it. She is not being taken advantage of by the male lover; she wants and chooses this interaction and revels in the closeness of it.

In its historical and social context, the Song of Songs is very similar to works from ancient Egypt and Mesopotamia about love between humans or anthropomorphized gods. In my favorite example of a love poem from ancient Mesopotamia, vegetables are allusions for sexual organs:

> He has sprouted, he has burgeoned, he is well-watered lettuce, my shaded garden of the desert, richly flourishing, his mother's favourite; he is well-watered lettuce; my grain lovely in beauty in its furrows, he is well-watered lettuce; my first-class fruitful apple tree, he is well-watered lettuce.[2]

Here, the growth of vegetables and grains is a helpful metaphor for the singer to explain how sexual organs morph during encounters. Additionally, lettuce is significant because some ancient cultures believed that lettuce was an aphrodisiac to make one perform untiringly!

All this to say, the words that a culture uses to refer to sexual acts and sexual pleasure, as well as what's even considered sexual, will vary widely and depend on the culture itself. As with all metaphors, figures of speech for sexual acts rely on a common background for the readers. For example, if I'm in a church group of crocheters, I'm less likely to use the language of bulldozers to make a point or teach a lesson than to draw on language from fiber arts involving yarn, crochet hooks, stitches, and so on. The language used for sex in the ancient world is no different. For people who lived their lives in tune with seasons of planting, growing, and harvesting, language from the natural world would've made perfect sense. It's cleverly alluring to turn the everyday into the sensual. Also, people were familiar with everyday items like bolts, doors, windows, and the like. That's the language we see in Song of Songs 5 as well, where the lover's entrance is to more than simply a previously locked room. Without going into great anatomical detail, the singers of the Song can give us an intimate portrait of their encounters.

The Song of Songs shows different kinds of sexual acts enjoyed by the lovers. Song of Songs 2:3–6 includes the joy of taste as one of the pleasures enjoyed by the lovers:

As an apple tree among the trees of the wood,
so is my beloved among young men,
With great delight I sat in his shadow,
and his fruit was sweet to my taste,
He brought me to the banqueting house,
and his intention toward me was love.
Sustain me with raisins,
refresh me with apples,
for I am faint with love.
O that his left hand were under my head
and that his right hand embraced me! (Songs 2:3–6)

In the richly agricultural society of ancient Israel, fruit seems a fruitful way (pun intended) to conceptualize the sensory pleasures of sexuality. If I were a betting woman, I'd say oral sex is the juicy topic on the menu here. The Song of Songs invites us to come to a deeper understanding of all the ways we can experience sensual joys with someone else. While many mature Christians might blush at the inclusion of such references to sexual pleasure, including not merely those that have procreative purposes but also those purely for arousal, the Bible doesn't seem to have the same scruples here, at all. The "fruits" of the male lover could be his sexual organs, which the female lover enjoys sampling.

How do we make sense of a scripture that seems to freely celebrate the many types of lovemaking that are available? This is not what many of us think about when we consider "biblical sexuality." How do we then understand what the Bible desires for us as far as sexual pleasure?

My conclusion is that the Bible is much less sexually squeamish than we think it is. Postmodern people are by no means the first to explore and enjoy sexual pleasures of different kinds. And, within limits of love and respect for ourselves and one another and the created world around us, it's possible to experience sexual fulfillment through sampling a range of what is available. Just like the female lover of the Song is unembarrassed to admit that she enjoys oral sex with her partner, we can explore how we can delight in intimate engagement.

Part of the question for Christians has been the Song's genre. Christians have tried to rationalize why this richly sexual book appears in the Bible. Historically, the church has stated that the Song of Songs is about the loving relationship between Christ and the church as his bride, building on older Jewish traditions of interpreting it as the relationship between God and Israel. Perhaps this ameliorates some of the raciness in the song—if sanitizing Song of Songs of its sexuality really is something we need to be about as believers! Many Christians understand the Song as a dialogue between Christ and the church, with the church as his holy bride. The Song is not, from this perspective, a model for the physicality of human relationships, but the union of the soul and God, or more corporately speaking, of Christ and his church. There's no extent to which Christ the bridegroom will not go to win the heart of his bride.

This is a perspective offensive to schools of Christian and post-Christian thought that want to emphasize and embrace the fleshly aspects of the song. Contemporary interpretations often criticize past perspectives that have overly spiritualized what is clearly a work about sex between human partners. Feminist scholars and theologians of the body have praised the Song for its seemingly progressive positions on sexuality and openness to exploring the body.[3] As a backlash against purity culture, the Song feels powerful. The proponents of this view tacitly or explicitly say, "Sex is good! The body is good!

Marriage isn't necessary for fulfilling sexual union!" This isn't really about God, they claim, but the celebration of how good bodies are when they come together.

From my perspective, I don't know why it can't be a bit of both, each perspective on the Song enriching the other. Yes, the Song describes human love, but in some respects, human love can be the closest approximation we have of the divine! The ecstasies of human fleshly love can actually be increased, in turn, by an understanding of how they mirror the divine. The two are inseparable.

This is something that Christian mystics have understood more fully than anyone else. When I was in college studying abroad in Italy, I had the opportunity to see the famous sculpture of Teresa of Avila, *The Ecstasy of St. Teresa*, created by Gian Lorenzo Bernini, in the Corano Chapel of Santa Maria della Vittoria in Rome. An angel is caught in the act of piercing Saint Teresa's heart. She is reclined, her eyes open slightly. Take away the sacred context, and it wouldn't be hard to imagine her in a much more amorous situation.

Teresa of Avila's writings tell a similar story. She describes the experience of being "penetrated" by an angel:

> Beside me, on the left hand, appeared an angel in bodily form. . . . He was not tall but short, and very beautiful; and his face was so aflame that he appeared to be one of the highest rank of angels, who seem to be all on fire. . . . In his hands I saw a great golden spear, and at the iron tip there appeared to be a point of fire. This he plunged into my heart several times so that it penetrated to my entrails. When he pulled it out, I felt that he took them with it, and left me utterly consumed by the great love of God. The pain was so severe that it made me utter several moans.

> The sweetness caused by this intense pain is so extreme that one cannot possibly wish it to cease, nor is one's soul then content with anything but God. This is not a physical, but a spiritual pain, though the body has some share in it—even a considerable share. So gentle is this wooing which takes place between God and the soul that if anyone thinks I am lying, I pray God in his goodness, to grant him some experience of it.[4]

Saint Teresa beautifully articulates how the veil between the physical and the spiritual is much thinner than we think it is. Divine love can recall the physical ecstasy of the interaction between lovers; sex between lovers can open us to the love of the divine. If divine love is the ultimate love, which I, alongside countless other Christians, believe that it is, then it encompasses all other loves, including the erotic. The only way to put something as profound as divine love into words is to reference things that are more familiar. Just as we pray to God, alongside Jesus, as "Abba, Father," just as Jesus tells us the parable of the Shepherd and Psalm 23 reminds us, "The LORD is my shepherd," just as God is the potter who shapes and molds us (Isaiah 64:8; Jeremiah 18, among others), so Jesus is also the lover of souls.

Many Christian groups have forgotten this in our haste to normalize sexuality within people. When I was in a church youth group in a progressive Protestant denomination, there was pushback from church leaders against "Jesus is my boyfriend" music. Sometimes, the lyrics of contemporary Christian music can feel so rapturous that it's unclear if the subject is Jesus or the hot date someone is pining over! My church's unease, as far as I can tell, was for two reasons. First, my church was heavily focused on social justice. "Jesus is my boyfriend" music neglected these themes, it seemed, because it focused more singularly on an individual relationship with Jesus. Second, I think, there was a discomfort at what seemed like an intermixing of divine spirit and human sexuality.

But Christianity is an incarnational religion. We believe in the Word made flesh. Jesus is the God-man who enters fully into human experience to overthrow the sin and death that hold us captive. Because of this, our experiences of sexuality are not divorced from the divine realm, but are, at their best, a pathway toward them.

Additionally, if Saint Theresa and other great mystics had revelations of divine presence that involved experiences of Christ as a lover, are we in a position to argue with them? These experiences of divine intimacy and the sensual are not meant to lead us away from social justice. Instead, they transform us so deeply that we cannot do otherwise than walk in the footsteps of the great Lover who served the last, the least, and the lost.

All this to say, the sensual isn't at odds with the revelation of God. Like the writings of Saint Theresa, Song of Songs, though it does not include the name of God directly, introduces us to the intermingling of divine and human love. Used right, pleasure shows us God's delight in us.

Sex, like so many other things in our world—money, technology, relationships, our own doctrines—can become an idol. Sex itself is not God. But a reasonable goal could be to experience sex in such a way that we become able to love God and our neighbor through the ways we explore and appropriately direct our sexual desires.

So how can sexual pleasure draw us into joyful obedience to the greatest commandment, to fully love God and our neighbor? This might seem like a nonstarter for a lot of

Christians. Pleasure is on the margins of what seems acceptable. Pleasure can feel like something scandalous or selfish. How can an understanding of pleasure possibly be part of the discipleship of Jesus?

Especially in committed partnerships, the ideal and healthy situation is for two people to be so focused on meeting each other's needs that everyone's needs are met. Historically, Christians have directed much more attention to men's sexual needs and desires than women's. Men's arousal and orgasm have delineated sex much more than those of women. But true servanthood in sexuality means that the comfort, pleasure, and ecstasy of sex is the concern of both parties. Sex is about giving *and* receiving, and the presence of both defines a healthy sexual relationship. In this type of relationship, we should be able to trust that our partners will, with our guidance as communicative partners, be eager to meet our sexual needs and respect our sexual boundaries. This trust frees us to focus on serving our partner through offering them the kinds of affection that will give them pleasure.

When each partner is able to give freely for the sake of the other to know love through the touch and affection of the other, both partners can be fully satisfied without being selfish. When we tune into one another in this way, *giving* one's partner pleasure becomes as pleasurable as receiving. This exchange of giving and receiving, and receiving becoming giving, becomes infinite. It mirrors what is called the *perichoresis* of the Trinity, where the mutual love of the Father and the Son gives rise to the Holy Spirit.

Put very bluntly, when we have sex with our spouse, it's important to ask ourselves, "Is the way I'm interacting with them in bed commensurate with their identity as a child of God, a beloved child of the King, for whom Christ died?"

And read the most charitable way that I can imagine, I think that might be what the Pauline writer is getting at when he talks about "submission" in Ephesians 5. Nope, it's not "submission" in the BDSM sense at all, but the idea that we put ourselves in each other's power when we choose to be sexually involved with another person. We give ourselves to one another, with a full knowledge of both the love given and the risk of being hurt, and we die to each other in the way Christ died for each of us.

Sexual pleasure isn't dirty or shameful. It's a gift of God. And it's meant, along with all the other difficult and worthy things we do in our lives, to lead us into the fulfillment of the best things that God can imagine for our lives. And that brings me back, once again, to the great commandment. As Christians, even and especially in our sexual pleasure, we're called to love our neighbor. This means that the kinds of pleasure we choose, and how we explore our sexuality, must always seek the good of our beloved. They must uplift the human person as created in the image of God. Pleasure can absolutely become destructive and selfish when it erodes the sanctity of human dignity.

This is what the Song of Songs teaches us. Over and over in the Song of Songs, the lovers tell us about pleasure, yes, but they return again and again to simple and profound mutuality: "I am my beloved's, and my beloved is mine" (Song of Songs 6:3). Pleasure within genuine intimacy allows us to give each other the greatest gift we can offer: ourselves. Sexuality is fulfilling when, and I'd argue *only* when, it involves sharing the gift of self. It's pleasurable when we are loved in such a safe way that we are free to give ourselves fully. When I am my beloved's and my beloved is mine, we reach the promise of Eden, to be "one flesh" with one another.

Put another way, pleasure isn't ever for its own sake, but to lead us into the first part of the great commandment: to come to know God and to love God, above all else. To wonder in the good creation that God has made. To exult in the love that God has created us for. To bless God for making us humans who can connect so intimately with each other that we become one flesh.

And rather than denying that this is the case, instead of suppressing it and allowing it to influence our interactions in unhealthy ways, we'd do better to acknowledge the need and desire for sexual pleasure.

8

Becoming Ourselves, Together

THE PEOPLE WE'VE AWAITED

Sexuality isn't just physical. Anyone who has been in a sexual relationship with someone else knows that it can be deeply emotional and spiritual as well. After all the discussion on knowing and loving ourselves apart from a relationship, it might seem like a quick about-face to talk about what it means to cultivate our selfhood *within* a relationship. I'll be the first to say that relationships are not easy. As I know from my own story, twice over, relationships and especially marriages can cause some of the deepest harm that we experience as people. But I still hold out the belief and hope that longstanding, committed relationships can be holy.

Sex is one of the ways that we can express the full gift of self to another. This gift is meaningful only if it's freely and unreservedly given. If we're forced in any way, it's not a gift anymore; it's theft. It's rape, including in marriage. If we have emotional reservations, it's not a full gift, either. If we're not prepared to share *all* of ourselves with each other, in the bedroom or out, I'm inclined to say the nature of the gift is different, too.

With a little trial and error, most people can find a way to have sex. But most don't, outside of committed relationships, learn how to make love. That requires something deeper, something more permanent, something more meaningful, than deriving pleasure through contact of reproductive organs. Honestly, for many people, after a little trial and error, the physical part is easy. What's a lot more difficult is growing the capacity to carry the weight of intimacy with another beloved child of God, supporting and celebrating them in the divinely given goodness that they bear. But that's what it takes to truly make love.

Sex gives us knowledge about another person. I think it's entirely appropriate how, in Hebrew, the word *yada*, "know," is also the word used for sexual intercourse. When we have sex we come to *know* someone. Parts of our body overlap and enter one another in an experience that exits the realm of everyday interactions.

Sex changes within long-term relationships. In time, it doesn't necessarily carry the same thrill and excitement as a new love. Sometimes, especially if we have kids, it gets trickier to reconnect. New parents are tired and grumpy and overwhelmed and often dealing with postpartum physical or mental health issues that can make sex physically more difficult to accomplish. As we get older, sex changes as well, as hormones can change and libido along with them. Physical limitations can mean a renegotiation of how we relate to each other. At my age, stage, and life experience, I don't know what that whole evolution is like. But I *do* know, having been a chaplain to seniors, that we never stop seeking profound connection to others, discerning who we are, and navigating relationships.

It's true that we don't always know what we're in for when we commit our lives to each other. Given my earlier experiences of broken marriage, I take marriage commitments all the more seriously. I didn't fully understand what I was entering into as a younger woman. The beauty of marriage is that when we say our vows, we are promising to love a person in all the ways the divine image of their selfhood manifests over time. Knowing that we won't get it right all (or even most) of the time. Knowing that the person they are today definitely is not going to be the person they are ten years from now, twenty years from now, fifty years from now. Knowing that some of the ways they change will be easier for us to accept, and others will be harder. Knowing that our own desires for how our partner should be won't mean that they change to be that way.

So we have to choose carefully! Because we can't control the outcome of a person's becoming in marriage (and nor should we be able to; in giving us free will, even God has relinquished that control). We can't ever know how someone is going to change, but in my experience of making big mistakes, here's a guideline I've developed for myself: *However a person is in even a small amount now, before a permanent commitment is finalized, they're likely to be in even bigger proportion later.*

I'll give an almost trivial example of myself, in the non-sexual arena. I struggle with anxiety, especially when there's chaos around me in the home environment. Laundry everywhere, unwashed dishes, kids running late for activities—I freak out, big time. I'm trying to work on myself, I really am. But left to my own devices, and without support and patience from those around me, I can easily get irritable and yell. Especially in my first marriage, this was probably a very difficult aspect of my personality for my partner to deal with! He seemed to be saddled with this frazzled and panicky version of Susannah that he totally didn't mean to marry. And it's understandable that he was frustrated by that.

Could he have known how anxious I'd become after having kids? Well, probably not really, and it wasn't his fault I became like that. But the biggest indication of how I'd act later in the marriage was probably how I was when we were dating. I was anxious running late to our church small group; I was panicky when I misplaced my keys. Small clues, to be sure, though not the whole picture.

My post-children anxiety was not the fault or responsibility of my children's father. The best he could've probably done, and maybe he did do, was to realize that the small indications that I was an anxious person *before* the marriage informed him that this tendency to panic would probably be magnified as I got older and experienced more stress from having children. There was a lot of work I needed to do on myself, too, and my partner wasn't responsible for that. All I mean to say is that what may start as small signs in dating can often expand greatly in marriage.

So as we're going through the process of dating and picking a partner, wisdom includes curiosity and openness to encounter all the features of our partner—which may be more difficult to discern during the honeymoon phase of a relationship. When it comes to sexuality, we may want to be aware of how our partner talks about boundaries and cheating. We may want to observe what they say about previous relationships and how those relationships started and ended. We may want to notice how open a partner is to discussing sexuality and how comfortable they are with their own body. We may especially want to note how lovingly a partner holds the places of vulnerability in our own stories. Are there any idiosyncrasies that shape the way they understand their relationship with sexuality?

It sounds like a truism, but people are what they are, and they like what they like. Especially after we become adults, it takes a lot of intention to change those things about ourselves. I know exceedingly few people who have had any luck getting a partner to change, or who have changed because a partner wanted them to. If we enter into a relationship believing that its success is reliant on a partner changing, we're probably bound for a lot of pain, and may cause it as well. As we observe a potential partner's behavior, we're not doing so to cast judgment or—as my elementary-age kids were taught to say about their peers' snacks—to "yuck someone else's yum." What really matters is how these things work in a relationship between two people who care about each other deeply but imperfectly. It's okay and even important to be honest with ourselves about how our partner's tastes shape us, and if they don't work for us! Saying no and calling things off in dating is hard, but it's harder being in a committed relationship and realizing that we are in way too deep for comfort.

Loving ourselves—the predecessor to loving our neighbor—means being discerning about whom we choose to date and marry. Loving our neighbor means bearing with one another even through the messy, hard, and awkward parts of being in relationship with each other. It means accepting that our neighbor is not perfect, and they are created to be their own being, glorifying God in their entirety, not there to merely serve our own sexual or relational ends. As couples in committed relationships, together we love God most of all by loving and caring for God's image in our neighbors closest to us in every way, including as we pursue sexual health and wholeness for each other and ourselves.

Our sexual selves evolve across a lifespan. And when we have a lifelong partner, the journey is one we take on together. In many Christian wedding liturgies, a passage from the book of Ruth figures prominently. These are not romantic words in the context, where Ruth declares her intention to stand beside her embittered mother-in-law no matter the cost:

> Do not press me to leave you,
> to turn back from following you!
> Where you go, I will go;
> where you lodge, I will lodge;
> your people shall be my people
> and your God my God.
> Where you die, I will die,
> and there will I be buried.
> May the LORD do thus to me,
> and more as well,
> if even death parts me from you! (Ruth 1:16–17)

My parents included this beautiful passage in their wedding ceremony as vows, and when I went to a wedding of a young couple recently, they too chose it as a reading from the Old Testament. These are words of dedication and commitment to love that transcend the circumstances.

And maybe it's appropriate that these words of commitment in these weddings hail from friendship. Because in the end, as far as I understand it, marriage is one of the deepest forms of human friendship we can have. A long friendship in which we give our whole lives, our whole selves to one another, in which we go deeper and broader the longer we share ourselves together.

Marriage is built to satisfy some of the deepest needs that we have as humans. The story of the first partnership, between the first couple, is built from the yearning we have to connect with another human that we know beyond all others, whom we can support and who supports us in turn. "It is not good to be alone," God says, and I believe it; there are few other spaces and means for humans to grow more than in a relationship with a human whom we are obligated to see and love every day, whether we wake up feeling like it or not.

In the second creation story of Genesis, the first couple is created one from the other. In this telling of the story, each begins simply as the generic Hebrew *ish* and *ishah* for "man" and "woman."

> Then the LORD God said, "It is not good that the man should be alone; I will make him a helper as his partner." So out of the ground the LORD God formed every animal of the field and every bird of the air and brought them to the man to see what he would call them, and whatever the man called every living creature, that was its name. The man gave names to all cattle and to the birds of the air and to every animal of the field, but for the man there was not found a helper as his partner. So the LORD God caused a deep sleep to fall upon the man, and he slept; then he took one of his ribs and closed up its place with flesh. And the rib that the LORD God had taken from the man he made into a woman and brought her to the man. Then the man said,
>
> "This at last is bone of my bones
> and flesh of my flesh;
> this one shall be called Woman,
> for out of Man this one was taken."
>
> Therefore a man leaves his father and his mother and clings to his wife, and they become one flesh. And the man and

his wife were both naked and were not ashamed. (Genesis 2:18–25)

Before this story, the first couple are simply generically referred to as "man" and "woman," *ish* and *ishah*. They get their proper names as Adam and Eve only when *both* of them are present in the second creation story. It isn't just that the woman is made from the man's rib; the man isn't called by his own proper name, Adam, until the woman is created, too. In this way, the two make each other into themselves.[1] In Genesis 3, Adam and Eve are named characters in the story, who, admittedly, immediately use their distinctiveness to wreak havoc in paradise. Sometimes, this story is taken in sexist directions, that women are defective men (say what?) or that men come first and therefore are more important. But I think this gets the story quite wrong. What if women are actually the pinnacle of creation, for starters, because God was saving the best for last? Or what if—and what I think is more likely—one another's presence causes us to fully realize who we are?

The man and woman are made of the same stuff. The man donates some of the raw materials for Eve's creation, but that's no reason his power and authority are held over hers. Rather, the point is that we are made of what is closest to one another's hearts. The man gives over a piece of himself for God to create the woman. There are few more beautiful examples I know of how marriage is a profound avenue of becoming more human together.

Because this is what we do when we choose to commit ourselves to building a life together, which presumably involves our sexuality as well. We give ourselves over to the building up of the other. This is not to surrender our dignity, our personhood, or our individuality. Living in Edenic paradise with one another means that everyone is supposed to enjoy the garden. But we share ourselves with each other so very profoundly that it could be that we are joining with God in the process of creating one another.

This idea squares with the great commandment. We are *loving* our partners as ourselves when we join together in building them out of the same stuff of which we are made. Through our love, we have the astonishing capability to co-create each other into even more of who we are born to be. We enliven the image of God within each other.

How can sexuality do this? How, through sexual intimacy, are we co-creating our partner?

What if the hands with which we touch one another could be hands of blessing, hands that confirm as protected and sacred what God has already declared good? What if the touch of our bodies could seal a covenant to seek the good of the other, continually, for our whole lives? What if the words of our mouths, even in the throes of passion, call out boldly what is beautiful and good and beloved? What if each kiss we give bestows the peace of Christ?

The good news is that all these things can be real and holy and true. The bad news (if we can even call it that) is that we might need to shape our interactions with a bit more intentionality.

What's beautiful about the Genesis 2 story is that it ends shamelessly. When we are so closely connected that we share our substance, the traditional barriers that keep us from knowing ourselves or others fully disintegrate. The couple is "naked and not ashamed."

Contrast this bold nakedness with what happens after Adam and Eve choose power over intimacy with God and one another in Genesis 3. After they eat from the tree of the knowledge of good and evil, they *realize* that they're naked, and they don't like it, either. Not only do they want to be clothed in front of each other, but confronting God doesn't feel like such a great idea to boot.

> Then the eyes of both were opened, and they knew that they were naked, and they sewed fig leaves together and made loincloths for themselves.
>
> They heard the sound of the LORD God walking in the garden at the time of the evening breeze, and the man and his wife hid themselves from the presence of the LORD God among the trees of the garden. But the LORD God called to the man and said to him, "Where are you?" He said, "I heard the sound of you in the garden, and I was afraid, because I was naked, and I hid myself." He said, "Who told you that you were naked?" (Genesis 3:7–11)

There's self-awareness that's good, but then there's the unwillingness to be seen because we believe the distorted message that we're not good enough, because we've wised up to how the world really works. Suddenly, being seen by each other and even by God doesn't feel safe or good, because we know that what might be seen isn't good enough.

Isn't it so indicative of the fall that where once we were together and whole and healthy, we are now separated by our own feelings of exposure? I think it's no mistake that Genesis tells this story of the fall as the disintegration of the closeness of a bonded couple like Adam and Eve. Seeking power and prestige over openness and vulnerability results in heartbreak, for God and for the humans. A barrier blocks our instincts to vulnerability.

I wonder when in our lives we are truly naked, and when we hide behind fig leaves to block ourselves from really experiencing intimacy. Where do we allow shame to block us from breathing deep into the love of another person and being known all the way? And what can help us to really get naked with one another, in the best sense?

A handful of people in the world have seen me naked—definitely more since I've gone through labor with my three girls. Before each of my girls' births, I worried about being naked, and I carefully packed special clothes to wear in the hospital or birth center—a sports bra, swim bottoms, even a special labor and delivery dress. But each time, I'm pretty sure I ended up stark naked by the time my girls were born, and by the time I got to that point, I'm pretty sure I didn't care, either. And it didn't matter to the midwives, nurses, or technicians, either—not to mention my brand-new baby. The opening of self that happens in key physical moments of our lives means that the modesty or even shame that so many of us experience is transcended. Instead of being held back by our internal constraints, we turn to another with joy, longing, and new life.

The rule of thumb for me is that if you *have* to turn off the lights to conceal your nakedness, it's probably not intimacy: it's just sexual intercourse. It's not making love. It's hiding from each other while paradoxically sharing your bodies in the most personal way there is to share a body. And that doesn't make sense.

What would happen if we gave ourselves the gift of having sex when we know someone so well that we're truly opening ourselves to them, truly prepared to allow ourselves to see and be seen in return?

When we're really prepared to experience sex not just as a vehicle for pleasure, not as a transactional exchange, everything can change. We can start to experience sex as a way to open ourselves to divine love, from which we can never really hide, either—just ask our friend Adam—and be forever changed. At the tail end of his famous love hymn, the apostle Paul writes about the barrier we experience as people who cannot fully know or be known in our current state of being: "Now we see only a reflection, as in a mirror, but then we will see face to face. Now I know only in part; then I will know fully, even as I have been fully known" (1 Corinthians 13:12).

Paul is most likely referring to the spiritual realm, but there's also a sense in which "knowing fully" and being known fully by another person prepares us to know God and echoes our relationship with God. We are called to relationships of godliness, in which the way we know and love each other prepares us to encounter the ultimate Knower. We are given the gift of intimacy—real intimacy, not the "let's do it with the lights off" variety—to be transformed by love.

Good sex is profoundly intimate, though it is only part of intimacy. We shouldn't ever make the mistake of confusing the physical act of sex alone with actual intimacy. Other human experiences can approach the intimacy of sex, if not surpass it. A dear friend told me once that crying in front of someone for the first time is like getting undressed in front of them for the first time—notice that even to explain the intimacy of weeping in front of someone else, she used the vocabulary of sexual intimacy.

Being known fully changes us. Being known fully allows us the freedom to be who we are most authentically while believing that we are also loved fully, exactly as we are. This is a potent combination, one that has the power to shape our lives for good, forever. Once we've known that kind of love, I don't think we ever really fully recover from it. Once it pierces us, we can never go back to living fully in the shadows, because someone has seen us, just as we really are.

Some people I know weep while they experience orgasm. And I think that's a beautiful thing. We cry when something touches us emotionally, and good sex can and should bring out some of the most powerful emotions that we have. We can weep sometimes when we feel so interpersonally connected that we realize we can never feel any closer to another human being, as long as we live. Sexuality mightily molds our emotions toward another person, and that is one of the reasons it is so powerful, regardless of whether we're among the lucky few who cry when we climax. One of the questions we should ask ourselves before getting sexually involved is, "Am I prepared to bear the deep emotions that may be awakened through a physical, emotional, and spiritual union with this person?"

Don't get me wrong. Especially in a culture where hookups can be a rite of passage for many emerging adults, it makes sense that, for some and maybe even many people, deep attachment is not the result of every sexual interaction. I also don't buy the purity culture idea that by sleeping with someone, we're giving a part of our soul away; our soul is ours to keep until we reach our eternal rest, in my understanding. But I do think that sexuality *can* awaken some of our deepest, most painful, and most joyful feelings, and it *can* create attachment with another person.

There may well be times in our lives when we're simply not ready to open the floodgates of really, genuinely, and fully sharing ourselves with another person. I think that's one of the stronger arguments of waiting for marriage to have sex. If we take sex not only seriously but also spiritually, we need to be prepared for how much knowing and being known can affect us. Sex is good, and to be shared, but it also makes us vulnerable. Whom do we trust enough to utterly share our bodies with? Whom should we? To whom do we offer the ultimate gift of self?

Marriage to me, in the holy ideal to which God calls married people, represents the gift of self in an environment of safety where we can flourish. Sexuality within marriage invites us to truly become ourselves together, over the span of the years that we are given to enjoy together. Within married sexuality, in the security of a covenantal, sacramental union, we are empowered to use sexuality to bring life to our beloved.

What a gift.

Conclusion

LOVE DIVINE, ALL LOVES EXCELLING

Whether what I've written here is convincing or not isn't my greatest concern. Honestly, I'm happy to be wrong about many things. My greatest hope is that this book opens conversations. There is so much that we need to talk about. I have huge dreams that the next generation of Christians, my daughters included, will grow up in a healthier way than I and so many of my generation did. Silence is not our friend when it comes to sexuality.

We need to talk about sexuality. We need to talk to children and youth about their bodies and touch that is and isn't okay. We need to start teaching consent at an early age. We need to use the correct terms for private areas of our bodies so children can communicate clearly if there's something going on that's not okay, to empower youth to hold boundaries and report abuse. We need to be aware of how technology is exposing our children to sexually inappropriate content at earlier and earlier ages, and how, for many children, the first teacher about sexuality they encounter is pornography or confusing information from peers rather than the loving advice of a trusted adult. We need to talk about how abstinence-only sexual education doesn't actually seem to stop kids from having sex.[1] We need to talk about how so many emerging adults don't really know how to navigate the world of dating and relationships with actual discernment. We need to talk about how, even in marriage, sex isn't often the intimate encounter we want it to be. There's a lot to cover.

This book barely peels back a single sheet, but I hope it initiates conversations about how we fully protect, celebrate, and embrace one of God's greatest gifts to us. It's okay, and *good*, even, for these conversations to happen in churches! What better place to discern together how God leads us and how we are to love one another?

Of all the things I want to share with Christians about how our discipleship takes shape through our faith, it comes down to this: Our faith matters deeply in how we choose to interact sexually with ourselves and others. But maybe we've been approaching the question of *how* it matters in ways that distract us from the main point. In fact, it isn't rules or regulations or dress codes or questions of "how far can we go?" or even rings that tell us how we should engage the world as sexual beings. It's instead the love of God poured out on each of us extravagantly. There are probably helpful components of all those conversations as we endeavor to live faithfully in the world while also being true to who we know ourselves to be as people with needs and desires.

But if we take the words of Jesus seriously, in the end, everything, in all aspects of our lives, comes down to the passage that I've referenced so often during this book's journey:

> When the Pharisees heard that he had silenced the Sadducees, they gathered together, and one of them, an expert in the law, asked him a question to test him. "Teacher, which commandment in the law is the greatest?" He said to him, "'You shall love the Lord your God with all your heart and with all your soul and with all your mind.' This is the greatest and first commandment. And a second is like it: 'You shall love your neighbor as yourself.' On these two commandments hang all the Law and the Prophets." (Matthew 22:34–40)

The path that Jesus invites us on involves centering love above all else. That, to me, is what is so profoundly freeing about a Christian understanding of sexuality. If we know at our core that we are so deeply loved that God will never let us go, then we can embody a love for ourselves, our neighbors, and even back to God that shapes the rest of our lives. This love is so powerful that it leaves no corner of our lives untouched. And this even extends to our sexuality.

So many of us have allowed things other than the love of God to shape how we embody our sexuality in our day-to-day living. It's not hard to understand why. Whether it was purity culture or MTV or even the searing comments of middle school peers that gave us painful understandings of what it means to be a sexual being in the world, it's never too late to recover what is our birthright: belovedness so deep and powerful that it extends to everyone else too.

At the homeless shelter where I work, I have a dear friend and coworker whose testimony is one of overcoming addiction and now guiding others on journeys of healing. When she prays at the start of our staff meetings, she almost always says something like, "Jesus, let your peace and love and healing grow in us and let it be so powerful that it overflows to everybody else in need of healing that we encounter." I think of my four-year-old daughter who insists on "helping" with the dishes and adds way too much dish soap so that the sink overflows with oodles of bubbles until the whole floor is soapy too.

The love that God offers to the world through sexuality is not dirty, nor shameful, nor cheap, nor easy. The love that God reveals in sexuality is nothing less than the love of the cross, the love of God poured out freely yet at a high price by total self-giving. One of my favorite hymns, written by the great hymnographer Charles Wesley, goes like this:

> Love divine, all loves excelling,
> Joy of Heav'n to Earth come down,
> Fix in us thy humble dwelling,
> All thy faithful mercies crown;
> Jesus, thou art all compassion,
> Pure, unbounded love thou art;
> Visit us with thy salvation,
> Enter ev'ry trembling heart.

Sexuality, when we experience it and share it as the full love of God, can represent "love divine, all loves excelling, joy of heaven to earth come down." This is not at *all* to say that sex is our religion and we don't need the Bible or church or community or revelation or any of those things! But sex, when shared generously and reverently, is a beautiful example of how abundant and extravagant and sweet and fierce the love of God is for us. Even in the intimate interaction between two flawed and broken humans, we can feel the "joy of heaven to earth come down" in a microcosm in the arms of someone who loves us.

To sum up everything from this journey, how do we ensure as much as we can that our sexual choices embody the love and grace of God? How can our lives be so overflowing of "love divine, all love excelling" that *even the way we exist as sexual beings* proclaims the gospel of a God who loves us so deeply that he would have died for any one of us?

We fulfill the great commandment by dwelling within Scripture and letting Scripture dwell in us. Scripture is full of all kinds of stories about sex, and they're not usually the ones we expect, either. The Bible is full of stories about people's messy encounters with sexuality, and most situations, as in real life, are not cut-and-dried. There are no perfect people in Scripture, except for the man Jesus Christ, and everybody's trying to figure their own stuff out, just like you and me. Scripture expects us not to be perfect (well, except possibly for that pesky injunction in Matthew 5:48 to "be perfect as your heavenly Father is perfect"), but rather to stay engaged with God and our neighbor and keep trying to figure our stuff out. It might take some time, and it might involve some crushing failures.

And if our stories do involve these things, well, we won't be all that different from Abraham, either, who *kept* passing off his wife as his sister to spare himself and endanger both his wife and the promise for his progeny. Not that I recommend that path. We won't be all that different from Jacob, who worked for seven years just to be paired with the wrong woman—super oops and super cringe. We won't be all that different from Tamar (the Genesis one), who seduced her father-in-law to prove a point and ended up being part of the greatest genealogy ever. We won't be that different from Paul, who was single but says he struggled with a mysterious thorn in his flesh. And if we're lucky, we won't be all that different from Mary, either, who was chosen to bear God into the world and said yes to this beautiful and sexually unorthodox calling, and who was potentially suspected of adultery by pretty much everyone, including her fiancé. (Thank goodness Joseph was clutch with the dreams, or who knows where the mother of God might've ended up.)

But the movement of Scripture is toward, always, the great commandment, that living our lives rooted in love for God and neighbor is all that matters. A great deal of the sex in the Bible, no matter how potentially unorthodox, leads us to Jesus, so the genealogies of the New Testament tell us, whose life is love wrapped up in human flesh. Love incarnate, love divine. No shame, just story upon story of how even the weirder moments of the Bible got us to a place of experiencing the Savior face-to-face. What if all the stories of our sexuality could lead us to Jesus, too, no matter how gnarly the paths that took us there? What if we model ourselves on that love, on that story, becoming and abiding as rooted in the stories of Scripture as it's possible to be? That might be the genesis of a healthy sexual ethic.

But we also need to cultivate ourselves, too, in every way we can figure out how. After all, the great commandment reminds us that each of us needs to "love [our] neighbor as [our]self." Self-love is a challenging journey for many of us, male and female, especially when we've been told for so much of our lives that because of X thing about us (or X, Y, *and* Z), we're not loveable and we don't matter. One of the greatest surprises of my maturing life is that even the popular people I felt most resentful of as an insecure young person were people who also struggled with self-image.

We're all humans assigned to the project of figuring out how to live authentically in the bodies and the minds and the emotional makeup that we were born into, facing the ample evidence that our uniqueness simply isn't welcome in many corners of the world. Learning to live with ourselves well is deeply interconnected with our sexuality, because sexuality may ask us to share the essence of who we are with another person in the most intimate way imaginable. How can we fully share ourselves when we feel distaste or even disgust for who we are?

I believe that a preliminary step toward healthy and whole sexuality is learning to love and appreciate the beautiful and unique ways in which God created us. This is one reason that I think, as a Christian parent, it behooves us and our children to encourage the next generation to wait to explore sexuality fully with a partner, because most of us don't really get a good grasp on who we are until we've had more formative life experiences, our brains have developed more, and we've had the chance to explore our needs and wants, likes and dislikes, and values and morality.

We have the hope of becoming "the trees planted by streams of water, which yield their fruit in its season, and their leaves do not wither" (Psalm 1:3). Trees can't control the weather. Trees can't control whether the rain fails to come and a drought strikes. So it's a lucky thing to be planted in the right spot. When we're fully grounded in our sexuality, we have the opportunity to flourish.

We might have lost some of the value of planting in our times. We might need to spend some more time finding the streams where we can position ourselves, where the living water is close to us so we never get thirsty for it, so we never try to quench our deepest thirsts from waters derived from a less pure source. Being just us for a while, to plant ourselves by the flowing waters of God's mercy, is a kind of justice. We owe it first to ourselves to be healthy-ish and whole-ish as individuals, to know ourselves before knowing others sexually. We may never get to completeness in this life, but we are worth the effort. We also *need* to know ourselves and love ourselves before we can approach loving our neighbor—platonically, sexually, or otherwise.

When we do feel ready to be in a serious relationship or marriage, we need to love ourselves and others by practicing good boundaries. This might seem paradoxical at first, because most people don't necessarily equate love and boundaries. But if a key component of love is respect, then I don't know any better way to show respect, and therefore love, than by having good boundaries. To really love someone, we need to know how to take care of them by honoring their needs. And if someone really loves us, they need to take care of us by honoring our needs. Obviously, there are limits to our abilities to do that. If my needs cause harm to somebody else or violate somebody else's boundaries—well, that's an obvious problem. It might be that my needs aren't reasonable for *anybody* to accommodate. I've had partners before whose articulated "needs" involved always being listened to, even when what they were saying involved calling me obscene names. That's obviously not a valid need that I could accommodate, nor that anyone should have to endure!

It may be that two partners aren't compatible because one of them can't (or won't) meet the other's need. For example, I'm a super cuddly person with my romantic partners. If someone has discomfort with a lot of physical touch and finds my desire for frequent cuddles intrusive (totally valid) and has more need for physical space, they're probably not going to be able to meet that need of mine and we should probably avoid involvement that's too deep—because we simply won't meet each other's needs adequately. Daily life would be like swaddling a baby in sandpaper. Boundaries should ideally be clear and compatible at the beginning of a relationship, but then again, we don't always know what we need in a relationship until we get into it. So ongoing conversation is invaluable to the ongoing health of both people.

Additionally, we each have the God-given right to name our yeses and nos, sexually and otherwise. These don't have to be fully known before a sexual relationship begins, either! For many people, their first sexual encounters may be ones of exploration where they don't even know what they're comfortable with. And it's okay for those boundaries to change and develop over time. *Consent can always be given or withdrawn.* Misconceptions about consent are, in my opinion, at the root of many perpetrators' violations of their victims. Even and especially in marriage, where our harmony should be full, it is an intense violation for one person to strip the other person of the power to say yes and no to sexual interactions.

We follow the great commandment by setting and respecting boundaries, because how can we love our neighbor if we don't really know where we stop and our neighbor begins? We need to respect the space between us to have authentic love for those nearest us. Just as we want and need to have the full respect of a partner in our relationships, we need to afford our partners the same dignity.

But when we reach that sweet spot of relational wellness, our relationship, paradoxically, also helps us become *more of ourselves*. When we know our own needs and desires and also our partner's needs and desires, and when we can hold healthy boundaries, that relationship gives space for each person to flourish more wholly as who God created them to be. Boundaries and self-knowledge are important predecessors to the relationship; they structure the relationship by giving a container in which everyone is free to be who they are most wholly. Within those limits and guidelines set by mutual trust and respect, there's room to grow and flourish. Children of the Good Shepherd, every one of us, need to be led by quiet waters, by green pastures, so we can be fully nourished and grow as we need to.

Sexuality is one way that we can fully approach the personhood that God has gifted us. Sexuality, at its best, celebrates that we are created for love and continually formed by another's love. Loving each other, we call each other by name into the fullness of our identity as beloved children of God. We caress each other and become one flesh in a holy embrace of goodness intertwining itself with even more goodness. We join ourselves to one another because we can recognize the divine light in each other, and it ignites us, in turn. And the love and embrace of a partner, each of us already knowing who we are in relation to God, calls us into even more goodness, even more love, and even more holiness.

We love our neighbor as ourselves through sexual intimacy when we invite our beloved to stand in the light of being known, exactly and authentically for who they are, and celebrate that "it is good." In a healthy, committed sexual relationship, we are constantly in a graced cycle of knowing and being known, loving and being loved, growing and being grown, until we help each other be fully embraced by the divine light that made us and calls us home.

And yes—sexuality is also about fun and pleasure. It can be easy, perhaps, to spiritualize sex into dimensions that connect us with divine love, but at the end of the day, it also simply can be very satisfying to activate our nerve endings in intimate parts of the body in that way. Christians have very often been awkward and unnatural about talking about sexual pleasure—but we need to remember that God created sex not purely for reproduction or for creating a new family unit, but also to give us joy! God loves us and knows that pleasure makes us happy. We worship a good God who delights in our delights and desires that we seek these pleasures in ways that uplift the human person.

For too long, large swaths of Christianity have stigmatized pleasure as something that separates us from God. The Bible itself, especially in the writings of Proverbs, Ecclesiastes, and the Song of Songs, recognizes that pleasure within our bodies and love of God are not at odds! These texts talk about pleasure not as something to scorn or be ashamed of, but as something to share with others in loving and faithful relationships. Not only is pleasure about fun, but pleasure is about experiencing and sharing the fullness of what it means to be created in God's image, through sharing our bodies with others. Pleasure gives us a new scope of understanding what it means to really be alive and loving God's good creation. Pleasure is temporary and fleeting, yes, but this too returns us to God, who is the solid foundation of our being, who does *not* shift and change, yet who gives us *today* to celebrate and enjoy.

Obviously, there are aspects of pleasure that we need to be wary of. We can seek pleasure selfishly, not seeking the good of the other, and turn people into objects. We can allow our interests to lead us away from what uplifts all people and into what degrades and turns us into less than what we are meant to be. That is why the great commandment provides us with such wise guidance as we seek to recognize healthy pleasure. We can ask ourselves, "Is what I am drawn to and how I am seeking pleasure commensurate with loving God? Is what I am drawn to and how I am seeking pleasure commensurate with loving my neighbor? And is what I am drawn to and how I am seeking pleasure truly loving and honoring myself as created in the image of God?"

I can't answer these questions about sexual pleasure for anyone but myself and it wouldn't really help anyone but myself if I elaborated much more. In the end, this is a prayerful conversation that each of us needs to have with God. My goal here is simply for us to understand the conversation about pleasure as a theological one. I really do believe that God *wants us* to think about pleasure and how we relate to our desires throughout our lives and in different contexts.

Loving our neighbors as ourselves in a sexual relationship can mean that each person seeks the pleasure of the other. This doesn't mean we neglect our own pleasure, but that we communicate openly about our needs, trusting in the faithfulness of our partner to meet them. We are invited, as faithfully committed people, to learn how to pleasure our partners as a way of loving and honoring them in the ways that they need and desire. And we can feel shameless and safely cherished when our partner takes the time and attention to learn how to pleasure us as well.

It's easy to idealize sex and imagine that it's something we're entitled to throughout our lives without any problems or concerns. Sadly, for many of us, our sex lives can be complicated. We can struggle at different times with sexual trauma, shame, dysfunction, or infidelity. Experiencing these struggles doesn't mean anything is wrong with us as people or that we're unworthy of experiencing sexual love! We may need and deserve the care of mental health providers, doctors, physical therapists, and other professionals to care for us as we navigate this difficult territory. I don't pretend to take the place of *any* of these important guides on our journeys to wholeness. However, I bring up these topics because it is so important that none of us think we are alone! God cares, the church really should care, and I care. These types of struggles are much more common than we are often led to believe. God is with us in them, and if the church is to model the love and care of that God, the church needs to join with its people in these struggles, too.

Sometimes, someone whom we deeply love may struggle with one or more of these deeply painful and personal issues. When this person is also our partner, it may be difficult to know how to love them well. When the issue also causes harm to us, it may be time to exercise our love and care by setting boundaries and possibly leaving the intimate relationship. This can be a difficult choice to make, but it can also be the best way toward freedom and life for both ourselves and those we love. At times, though, it may *not* be difficult to make the choice to end a relationship for ourselves and those we love. I recently questioned a friend for automatically saying "I'm sorry" upon learning that an acquaintance had gotten divorced. Divorce and other endings of relationships can be openings into celebrating wholeness and new life, even as we linger in the sorrow of what can no longer be. And it's okay to feel joy *or* sorrow, or even both, if we need to walk away to empower the flourishing of life for all parties in the relationship.

But there also are circumstances where we are *not* being harmed through another person's actions, where we are called to journey alongside our partners as they search for wholeness, including healing from past trauma, confronting their wounds, and dealing with difficult conditions and diagnoses that affect them as sexual beings. This is why it is so important that our sexual love for our partner is held within a broader love, of God-given agape love, for us to be able to meaningfully extend care. If we are in a relationship just because we feel sexual love or lust for another person (which, of course, isn't the same as love), our relationship is likely headed for a painful conclusion. A relationship where we are truly loving our neighbors as ourselves calls us to exercise that love even when the sexual part of the relationship is not easy, or nonexistent.

When we cannot perform sexually, for whatever reason, we're also called to extend this same love and care to ourselves. Again, we can't really love our neighbor until we've reached a deep comfort and wellness with ourselves in our own bodies, minds, and spirits. This can take time and space, but it's so worthwhile to make the journey.

* * *

My hope is for all of us to know that our sexuality is held within the love of God and belongs, as we do in all our being, to God. But we also belong to one another when we pledge our commitment to someone. There are no special rules about sexuality that we need to learn and follow as Christians. There's simply a knowledge that to live as whole sexual beings, the same compassion and love we rely on from God in all other areas of our lives should extend to our sexuality, as well.

We must live our lives in love with God to live sexually well. It's not enough to compartmentalize our love of God to places in our lives where it's easy, convenient, or not awkward. It's not enough to love God in the places of our lives we're ready to share with the divine. God wants to meet us in all the places in our lives, and for us to offer every act of our lives—including the sexual ones—as acts of worship to an ultimate Love so much greater than we are.

We must live our lives in love with our neighbors—the neighbors that we know, the neighbors we do not know, the neighbors we love, the neighbors we have yet to love. Our sexuality, insofar as we choose to live it out in relationship with others, needs to honor and respect the dignity of each person. If we love our neighbors, we will share the gospel with them. We need to live our lives sexually so that even this aspect of our lives proclaims the gospel to our neighbors—of a self-sacrificing, gentle and kind, passionate love of a Christ who relinquished his life for us. If our neighbors were to observe our sexuality—as witnessed through our relationships with ourselves, our significant others, and even our respect for strangers—does this part of our lives proclaim the gospel?

Sexuality is God's gift to us, a manifestation of God's grace that we now have the free will to live out in the world. Figuring out how to do that is not necessarily the easiest business, but God is with us in it. We do not need to be afraid, because God's grace abounds in us. God has loved us so deeply—first, preemptively, with initiative—that how could we do any less than to strive to live out God's love through our sexuality? How can we do any less than strive to make the great commandment our habit of daily living?

It is a *gift* to have these teachings from Jesus, not a legalistic trap to condemn us to blind obedience for the rest of our lives. It is a *gift* to be empowered to live our lives in such deep love for the One who created us and for those who surround us. Sexuality is not the whole puzzle of how we do this, but it is a piece of the puzzle, and a beautiful one at that.

My hope and prayer for all who read this book is this:

May God, who gave us sexuality, fill us with the grace to share it and live it out purely and beautifully with those to whom we are most deeply committed.

May God heal us from all the ways that painful teachings and past traumas and physical ailments limit us from full enjoyment.

May God fill us with the grace to teach emerging generations with more openness and grace than that with which we were taught.

May God fill us with the grace to be faithful and just in all the ways our sexuality manifests itself in the world.

Amen.

Notes

FOREWORD

1. Sheila Wray Gregoire and Dr. Keith Gregoire, *The Good Guy's Guide to Great Sex: Because Good Guys Make the Best Lovers* (Zondervan, 2022), 149.
2. See Sheila Wray Gregoire, Rebecca Gregoire Lindenbach, and Joanna Sawatsky, *The Great Sex Rescue: The Lies You've Been Taught and How to Recover What God Intended* (Baker Books, 2021), chaps. 3 and 10 for in-depth discussions of sexual pain disorders.
3. Gregoire, Lindenbach, and Sawatsky, 42.

INTRODUCTION

1. For a fuller exploration of the history of purity culture and its influence in North American evangelicalism, I recommend Jessica Valenti, *The Purity Myth: How America's Obsession with Virginity is Hurting Young Women* (Seal Press, 2009). For an excellent exploration of the psychological impact of purity culture and how we can recover from it, see Dr. Camden Morgante, *Recovering from Purity Culture: Dismantle the Myths, Reject Shame-Based Sexuality, and Move Forward in Your Faith* (Baker Books, 2024).
2. A wonderful starting point for exploring research on sexuality is Sheila Gregoire, *The Great Sex Rescue: The Lies You've Been Taught and How to Recover What God Intended* (Baker Books, 2021).

CHAPTER 2

1. There have been a number of scholars who have discussed this idea, which is suggested in the Talmud as well. Bart Ehrman's blog discusses this theory in a few different posts, as a tombstone of a "Pantera" appears to some to align with the Talmud's claims. There's a lively discussion on each side of this debate.

2. This is an ongoing discussion, and it's important to look at where the research is coming from as we evaluate sources (as is the case with any topic!). One useful resource in surveying some of the work on this topic is Rose Wesche et al., "Early Sexual Initiation and Mental Health: A Fleeting Association or Enduring Change?" *Journal of Research on Adolescence* 27, no. 3 (2017): 611–627.

CHAPTER 3

1. Teresa of Avila, *The Life of St. Teresa of Jesus, of the Order of Our Lady of Carmel*, 3rd ed. trans. David Lewis, available at https://www.gutenberg.org/files/8120/8120-h/8120-h.htm#l29.0.

CHAPTER 5

1. Mary Douglas, *Purity and Danger: An Analysis of Concepts of Pollution and Taboo* (Routledge, 2009), 44. First published 1966.

CHAPTER 6

1. RAINN, "Statistics: Perpetrators of Sexual Violence," last modified August 28, 2025, https://rainn.org/facts-statistics-the-scope-of-the-problem/statistics-perpetrators-of-sexual-violence/.

CHAPTER 7

1. The Church of England, "The Form of Solemnization of Matrimony," https://www.churchofengland.org/prayer-and-worship/worship-texts-and-resources/book-common-prayer/form-solemnization-matrimony.
2. "The Song of Lettuce: A Balbale to Inana and Dumuzid (Dumuzid-Inana E): composite text," *The Electronic Text Corpus of Sumerian Literature* (University of Oxford, 1999), https://etcsl.orinst.ox.ac.uk/section4/tr40805.htm.
3. See, for example, essays in *The Song of Songs: A Feminist Companion to the Bible*, ed. Athalya Brenner-Idan (Sheffield Academic Press, 2000).
4. Teresa of Avila, *The Life of St. Teresa of Jesus, of the Order of Our Lady of Carmel*, 3rd ed. trans. David Lewis, available at https://www.gutenberg.org/files/8120/8120-h/8120-h.htm#l29.0.

CHAPTER 8

1. My reading of Genesis 2–3 owes greatly to Phyllis Trible's groundbreaking essay, "Eve and Adam: Genesis 2–3 Reread," *Womanspirit Rising: A Feminist Reader in Religion* (1992): 74–83.

CONCLUSION

1. See, for example, "Abstinence-Only Education is a Failure," *Columbia University Irving Medical Center*, August 22, 2017, https://www.publichealth.columbia.edu/news/abstinence-only-education-failure.

The Author

Susannah Larry, PhD, is a chaplain, advocate, and writer who seeks to embody the way of Jesus in the beautiful and broken world that he loves. The author of *Forgiveness after Trauma* and *Leaving Silence*, Larry has a passion for bringing biblical theology together with contemporary experience. While she loves preaching, writing, and helping others make meaning in their own stories, the center of her world is her family. She resides with her family in Mishawaka, Indiana.